LUNAR
ASTROLOGY

BY THE SAME AUTHOR:

L'utilisation du Tarot en Astrologie Judiciare (The Use of the Tarot in Judiciary Astrology) 1933.

Les Astres Parlent (The Stars Speak) 1933.

La Symbolisme de la Vie Légendaire de Moïse (The Symbolism of the Legendary Life of Moses) 1933.

Les Rêves et les Astres (Dreams and the Stars) 1935.

Astrology Lunaire (Lunar Astrology) 1936 & 1947.

La Technique des Révolutions Solaires (Technique of Solar Revolutions) 1937. Second edition revised and augmented 1946. Third edition revised and augmented 1972.

Soyez-vous-même votre Astrologue (Be your own Astrologer) 1940.

Le Maître de Nativité (The Ruler of the Nativity) 1946. Second edition revised and augmented 1970.

L'Astrologie chez les Mayas et les Aztèques (Astrology among the Mayas and the Aztecs) 1946.

Esotérisme de l'Astrologie (Esotericism in Astrology) 1953.

L'Interprétation Astrologique des Rêves (Astrological Interpretation of Dreams) 1953.

Journal d'un Astrologue (Diary of an Astrologer) 1957.

Le Symbolisme de l'Aigle (The Symbolism of the Eagle) 1960.

A. VOLGUINE

LUNAR ASTROLOGY

An attempt at a reconstruction of the
ancient astrological system.

Translated by John Broglio

ASI Publishers Inc.
127 Madison Avenue
N.Y., N.Y. 10016

First published in French under the title *Astrologie Lunaire* in 1936

Fourth Edition copyright © 1972 by Alexandre Volguine

English translation copyright © 1974 by ASI Publishers Inc.

ISBN: 0-88231-004-6
LCC#: 74-75523

ASI PUBLISHERS INC.
127 Madison Avenue
New York, N.Y. 10016

Typeset in 11 point Baskerville
by dcmj, New York, N.Y. 10014

Printed in U.S.A. by
Noble Offset Printers
New York, N.Y. 10003

To Monsieur Nicolas, Affectionately.
A. V.

TABLE OF CONTENTS

ILLUSTRATIONS

PREFACE

Will this book by Alexander Volguine add something to Astrology? that is, some original and even indispensable element? I can reply without hesitation: Yes! Absolutely! Yes, without the slightest doubt!

It is deplorable that so many "texts of modern Astrology" shamelessly copy their predecessors, usually duplicating more error than truth. Volguine could never succumb to this fault: every single one of his books is truly individual, an original product of his own researches and conscientious thought.

I have described Volguine's work in my preface to the American edition of *The Ruler of the Nativity* (ASI PUBLISHERS INC., New York). I cannot recommend strongly enough that every English-speaking astrologer acquire this book; it is a *must,* which will open new horizons. It teaches an intelligent technique for calculating the strength of each planet in a given chart.

With the collaboration of ASI PUBLISHERS INC., we have also already prepared English editions of other essential works of Volguine for immediate publication: *Planetary In-Betweenities, The Astrological Parts, The Technique of Solar Returns.* I want to emphasize that these three books have no equivalent in the English *or* French astrological literature; and I am sure that our English-speaking readers will be enthusiastic in their response to them.

But let us discuss the present work:

In many ways Astrology in the west is not very consistent with itself. First it flatters itself that it is heir to the great Hermetic philosophers of ages past, and then it makes outrageous mockery of the great universal laws that every Initiate considers sacred and immutable Truths. Or where it recognizes these cosmic laws, it refuses to accept the conclusions which must follow *ipso facto.* And if it accepts some of them, they end up in flagrant contradiction with each other. I offer some random but undeniable facts:

1. Since our literature in the west is overstuffed with material

about Lilith, Lulu, the Dark Moon and others (which is usually imaginative speculation, moreover based on ephemerides which are not in agreement with each other), strangely enough, in retaliation we neglect a whole astrological system based on the Moon itself.

2. We recommend — at least in France — a very useful technique known as the Nodal Chart, which is done by transposing a given chart by subtracting the longitude of the Moon's North Node from the respective longitudes of all the cusps and planets in the chart — in other words, we permit ourselves to use a fictional point for erecting a new astrological chart. But we do not take the time to do the same for the very real Moon! Is it inconsistency or negligence? In any case, it is stupefying!

3. All our monthly prediction magazines are based on the Lunations, and discuss matters in terms of them; hence, the Sun/Moon combination. But very rarely does one discuss Lunar Astrology, and books that specialize in this branch of Astrology are even rarer. In one place we recognize the importance of the combination of the luminaries, and elsewhere we separate them and neglect one of the two members of this union.

4. For centuries the Trutine of Hermes has been promoted, both for the casting of the prenatal chart and for the rectification of the natal chart. Now this is all based essentially on the position of the Moon at different times of a woman's life. So we accept the determinative significance of the Moon before birth and during prenancy . . . but then from that moment on during the whole life of the individual, we very curiously neglect Lunar Astrology!

5. We maintain the fundamental aphorism: "The Sun and the Moon, after God, rule the Earth" . . . and yet we practice a truncated application of this law — a solar Astrology, cut off from its complement, Lunar Astrology!

6. In the directions we call "secondary" or "progressed," the passage of the Moon through the different Houses of the horoscope has very great significance since to a great extent it colors the principle orientation of the life from year to year. We have even developed a directional system called "Directions by Embolismic Lunation," but, very paradoxically, we do not use Lunar Astrology.

But above all, by neglecting Lunar Astrology we violate two great *Esoteric Laws,* which can be found in the Hermetic treatise, *The Kybalion*:

a. *Principle of polarity*: "Everything is Dual; everything has poles; everything has its pair of opposites; like and unlike are the same; opposites are identical in nature, but different in degree; extremes meet; all truths are but half-truths; all paradoxes may be reconciled."

b. *Principle of Gender*: "Gender is in everything; everything has its Masculine and Feminine Principles; Gender manifests on all planes."

Whatever does not respect these two laws of Hermetic Science ceases to be in accord with divine wisdom. In other words, solar Astrology inevitably demands an indispensable complement, Lunar Astrology; without which it is cut in half, in violation of the sacred laws, and hence conducive to error. There can be no Greater without a Less, no Yang without a Yin, no day without night, no masculine without feminine, no sun without moon, no solar Astrology without Lunar Astrology.

By rejecting Lunar Astrology, astrologers in the west — and only in the west — increase the state of error under which they labor. I repeat: only in the west. Neither the Hindu, nor the Chinese, nor the Arabian astrologer would omit extensive practice of Lunar Astrology. Here Oriental systems demonstrate more logic and sense; they operate in harmony with cosmological laws; they respect the sacred tradition that has come to us from the Great Initiates.

No Hindu astrologer would be content to analyze a chart with a solar approach alone. Even a beginner would be incapable of such heresy. Everyone — always — examines the solar chart *in obligatory close correlation* with its counterpart, the lunar chart. This is the Hindu doctrine:

1. An examination of Hindu astrological literature of the last twenty or thirty centuries will suffice to convince anyone of the central significance the great Rishis accorded to the Moon. Sometimes it seems that the Moon occupies the predominant place.

2. In all the Hindu texts, in all the periodicals, predictions based on the transits, or *Gochara,* are always and without exception determined from the sign occupied by the Moon, or the Lunar Ascendant (*Janma Lagna*), not from the Sun Sign, as in the west, nor even from the Rising Sign.

3. No astrologer will designate a new-born by his Sun Sign, or even by his Rising Sign, but by the constellation (nakshatra) occupied by the Moon. If you have the Sun in Pisces, Ascendant in Gemini, and the Moon in 25° 30' Libra (constellation *Vishaka* ruled by Jupiter), you would be called, in the west, a "Pisces," or better, "Pisces, Gemini rising." The Hindu astrologer will say that you were born in the *Vi-*

shaka nakshatra. Of course, he will add that your Ascendant is in Gemini, but only occasionally will he mention your Sun Sign.

4. Always and without exception, the Hindu astrologer will examine a given chart, even a horary or questionary chart, according to the two systems — solar and lunar — simultaneously. He will not need to draw up the lunar chart because he is accustomed to reading it at a glance by considering the House where the Moon is as the Lunar First House or Lunar Ascendant. He will mold his interpretation by passing from one to the other: the lunar chart will correct and in some way or other modify the interpretation of the traditional solar chart, even taking precedence over the latter whenever the coefficient of the Moon is higher. In any case — I repeat — never, but never, will the Hindu astrologer neglect to blend the two charts — solar and lunar, one forming the counterpart of the other.

I want to pause for a moment to insist once more on this point: the western astrologer should acquire the same habit — which will quickly become automatic — of drawing up and placing side by side the traditional solar chart and its lunar transposition. By continuing unreasonably to reject Lunar Astrology, the western astrologer operates in violation of the great esoteric laws.

5. Another important note: all Hindu directional methods (DASA) are calculated from the position of the natal Moon, and this holds true for *all* the planets. In other words, the Moon ordains the structuring of the directions for the rest of the chart, *including even the Sun.* This in itself speaks volumes. Would we dare say that at least forty centuries of Hindu Astrology consist of nothing but fantasy and error?

6. The comparison of charts, e.g., for a marriage, is based primarily on the position of the Moon by Sign, constellation, navamsa, etc., respectively for those to be wed, judged according to a series of criteria based on the two Moons.

7. All the Hindu almanacs daily note the *Tithis,* the distance between the Moon and the Sun; to a great extent these Tithis determine the favorable and unfavorable days for various activities.

In an election situation (*Muhurta*), the Hindu astrologer will by no means be stopped by a square or opposition, even one that we would consider clearly malefic; not only because his doctrine of aspects is totally different from ours, but moreover because he gives primary attention to the Tithis, to the position of the Moon by Sign, House, nakshatra, navamsa, etc.

For the two years I have been in India, I have been shocked by the number of marriages I have seen set by reputable astrologers for the very day of violent squares and oppositions, even involving malefics.

Recently I went to great lengths to modify the date of a marriage set for the same day as a Mars/Saturn square, for a person whose natal chart — of course — had a Mars/Saturn conjunction. I was made fun of and told: "What of that? The Moon is brilliantly placed and aspected!" I should make it quite clear that I by no means share this point of view, although I am an enthusiastic admirer of Hindu Astrology.

I recall that several years ago, the marriage date for a great Oriental sovereign (still alive and married), which was carefully determined by the palace astrologers, astounded the Occidental astrological world because it involved a violent configuration between two planets, one of which was a trans-Saturnian. Must we imagine that the astrologers missed it? Of course not. But the Moon was exalted, in a very favorable constellation and navamsa, in a good House and with good aspects. Still I must reiterate: although a firm believer in Lunar Astrology, I cannot subscribe to a thesis that bypasses our squares and oppositions.

8. All the Hindu texts indicate that afflictions to the Moon are very severely judged. If the Sun is the Atman, reflection of the Spiritual Sun, the Moon is *Chitta,* Mind and Soul. It is "karaka" (significator) of the mother (and the wife in the western system), prosperity, the favor of the great, etc. On its strength or weakness, position, afflictions, etc., depend fertility, longevity, and above all, the *Balaristha* or premature death of the new-born.

9. The notion of *Sade Sathi* and *Asthama Sani,* which I mentioned in a French article published in Volguine's *Cahiers Astrologiques* (#158, May-June, 1972, p. 135), covers the malefic results of a transit by Saturn through the Sign occupied by the Moon, and through the twelfth, second and eighth Sign from this one. These are very trying times in the native's life. As you can see, the calculation is based on the Moon and not on the Ascendant or Sun Sign.

10. Among their twenty-one subdivisions of a Sign or of the Zodiac (*Shodasavargas*) there is one called *Bhamsa* which divides the Sign into 27 parts of $1°\ 06'49''$ each, and which permits a more specific judgment of the native's strength and energy. Here again we encounter the division into 27 (or 28) parts, echoing the Mansions and the Houses of the Lunar Zodiac.

11. Of the approximately three hundred major *Yoga* (planetary combinations more or less equivalent to "super-aspects"), those in-

volving or based on the Moon are very numerous.

12. In the area of medical astrology, the Moon is a primary factor in vitality, good health (especially in a feminine chart), it indicates illnesses, it is implicated in cases of surgical intervention, it is considered very important in beginning a treatment, and even our ancient texts recommend not beginning either surgery or treatment during the fifteen days of the waning Moon. How could so many concepts be lost in our day — and solely in western Astrology?

I have cited only a few of the facts that demonstrate the importance of Lunar Astrology. I can cite others, connected with esotericism, iconography, mythology, or religion (the crescent of Islam, etc.). Here are a few:

13. There are multiple Sanskrit designations for the Moon: Sudhansu, Sudhakara, Sudhanidi, Amrita-Soo, Chandra, etc. . . . All carry the sense that it is the *life principle*. The lunar principle is *Soma*. By suppressing Lunar Astrology, we cut Astrology off from one of its two life principles, we mutilate and distort it.

14. In the *Yoga Shastras,* one of the *nadis* that carry Prana is called *Chandra Nadi*; the chakra between the eyebrows is called *Chandra-Mandala*. It is not only ridiculous, it is insane to imagine *Ida* without *Pingala* or *Pingala* without *Ida* (the two channels to the right and left of *Sushumna*; it would create a fatal imbalance . . . By analogy, do we not cause an equal imbalance in astrological interpretation by neglecting *Chandra*, the Moon, analogous to *Ida?*

15. In an old grimoire, the *Bhunavanadipika,* it is said that in every horoscope, the Moon is the Seed, the Ascendant the Flower, the navamsa, the Fruit (which ,coincidentally, indicates the importance of *Navamsa* in Astrology, unfortunately almost totally unknown to western astrologers). How could we neglect the Moon, which is the "seed"? The word "seed" seems very well chosen since we admit the Moon takes decisive precedence over the Sun in the determination of fecundation in a woman, and for the calculation of the prenatal chart, and that it rules all the calculations for chart rectification. Are we being consistent with ourselves?

But how can we explain the western astrologer's abandonment of Lunar Astrology? Quite simply through a crass and trivial motive: commercialism. It is the result of commercialism that marketers of horoscopic rags, who want to make the most money in the least amount of time, no longer have — time! So they sacrifice, they prune, they disfigure Astrology. The Parts? Get rid of them! The terms and decans? Get rid of them! The Moon's Nodes? Get rid of them! Primary directions? No way . . . too long, too difficult, no time, get rid of them! Dodecatemories? Ridiculous, get rid of them! The monomeres? (Truly a veritable jewel of Astrology.) Nonsense, they tell us, get rid of them, too! Do not laugh, dear reader. In the west, a few years ago we arrived at the point of getting rid of the Houses themselves — as if the millenia of Astrology that preceded us had been done by imbeciles! There is even talk of getting rid of the twelve Signs of the Zodiac . . . since someone recently claimed that there are "not twelve but thirteen." Why not! Why not get rid of the ten planets and use marbles! This is "modern Astrology" that claims to be scientific!

And since it is the so-called "scientific professionals" who lead the dance to a great extent and who have a great influence on the multitudes known as "amateurs," whom I prefer to call "non-commercial," it follows that the latter have ended up in spite of themselves by imitating their elders over the years. If some amateurs still cast Lunar Returns, how many professionals can you find that use them?

Nevertheless, an assiduous and impartial experimentation with the Lunar Return has given sufficient proof of the value of this method; and it is fervently hoped that astrologers will restore it to its rightful place. Perseverance brings its own rewards. On my own I have made some amazing discoveries, especially with anticipated events that occurred on the day of the exact transit of a given planet over the Ascendant, or Midheaven, Sun, Venus, etc., of the Lunar Return.

I also recommend casting Demi-Lunar Returns, valid for a two week period, i.e., charts for the moment in a month when the Moon transits the point exactly opposite its natal longitude. They can be of substantial assitance especially for discerning or for specifying the condition of a future event.

I believe a Solar Return *cannot be* reliably interpreted if it is not completed by the twelve Lunar Returns — or at least the more important ones among them. The Solar Return is like a "general x-ray," the Lunar Returns are "localized x-rays" — more specific, more probing, showing the condition of month after month, within the overall framework of the Solar Return.*

The preceding thoughts show clearly the extent of Volguine's achievement in having revived Lunar Astrology in the west, and with

---

*Along the same line, but let it be said only parenthetically, I have often wondered if the Solar Return may more specifically concern only the first half of the year, and if it would profit by being matched by a Demi-Solar Return, i.e., one cast for the moment when the sun transits in exact opposition to its natal longitude. This second Demi-Return would seem to pertain more specifically to the second half of the year, or at least would interpenetrate with the first and clarify it.

such masterly erudition as he demonstrates in the present work. In all of the occidental and oriental literature, including Hindu literature, it is absolutely the only text on Lunar Astrology ever published that is so complete and impartial; the only one that describes not only the twenty-eight Lunar Mansions (more or less equivalent to the Hindu *Nakshatras*), but also the twenty-eight Lunar Houses (which more or less correspond to the Hindu *Tithis*); the only one that gives the descriptions according to the Hindu asterisms, the *Manazils* of the Arabs, the Chinese *Siu,* and according to the Kabbala or Hebraic esoteric tradition. Not content with supplying us with all this knowledge, it is the only one, lastly, which has taken it as a point of honor to support it with a multitude of examples, almost all of them modern. To sum it all up: this book is a mine of information, undoubtedly the best we possess on the subject of Lunar Astrology, *not confined to one system,* and ignoring others. How many times I have verified the accuracy of these significations given by Volguine, and the reliability of the descriptions — all of which implies an extremely conscientious research.

Special thanks to Volguine for having set aside a separate chapter for Hecate, and for having noted that Hecate (the close conjunction of the luminaries) *has nothing to do with Lilith or Lulu.* This observation is essential. Hecate, or the Dark Moon, is *neither Lilith nor Lulu.* But how many people confuse the Dark Moon and Lilith!!

I have acquired the habit of always marking with a pencil dot the degree of the Zodiac where prenatal and postnatal Hecate occurred, i.e., the exact Sun/Moon conjunction immediately preceding and following the day of birth, and I also shade in the whole area eight degrees to the left and eight degrees to the right of this point. As regards this area I have occasionally made some curious observations, which must be pursued and analyzed. The degree and the whole zone of sixteen degrees (distributed equally to the left and right of the point) darkened by prenatal and postnatal Hecate are useful to note in transits, especially if the area is occupied by a planet. But let us not make a hurried generalization on the basis of one observation.

I would like to make a further suggestion: I feel that *each and every one* of the other nine planets must undergo some coloration through the influences of the Lunar Mansion it occupies, as they have been described by Volguine in this book. I am sure that there is some validity to this point of view. It would not seem logical to me that a planet could remain impermeable to even the general potential coloration of a given Mansion.

On the other hand, I believe that it is important to orient in order of priority the significations given by Volguine first, according to the significance to the rulership the Moon exercises in the chart, second, according to the significance of the House of the horoscope it occupies, and lastly, according to the significance of its aspects. For example, if the Moon rules or is in the Second House, and if among the attributes cited by Volguine there are some that involve the financial life, it seems reasonable to give some priority to these, and to assume that this area of influence will prevail during the life of the native. If the Moon is unfavorably aspected, this reinforces the risks or diminishes the luck on the financial level as indicated by the author. In the opposite case, these risks could be more or less decreased and the luck more or less intensified.

Does oriental Astrology — especially Hindu Astrology — give too pre-eminent a place to the Moon? I do not know . . . I do not think so! But one thing is absolutely sure in contrast: western Astrology has practically consigned the Lunar system to the junkpile. Common sense demands a return to a *golden mean,* that respects the great esoteric laws, and results in a harmonious marriage of solar and lunar Astrology. This book will be a great and undoubtedly outstanding contribution to this.

I will go one step further: even oriental astrologers — Hindu, Chinese, Iranian, Arabian, or others — have gained much, now that they have available an English edition accessible to their understanding, that they can study and use in daily practice; since, as I noted before, it supplies interpretations produced *by different systems.* Obviously the Hindu astrologer, for example, knows the meanings of his nakshatras, but he may not be well versed in the parallel significations in the Chinese or Arabian, or Hebrew system; likewise for the Arabian, or Iranian, or Kabbalistic astrologer, etc. . . .

I am sure that every objective, impartial astrologer with devotion and reverence for Astrology, will congratulate Volguine on his work, which offers something undeniably original and essential.

I will conclude by assuring the reader that the condition of the natal Moon by Sign, House, constellation, navamsa, etc., as well as by aspectual connections with various other planets, is an indispensable primary consideration in Spiritual Astrology.

I wish the greatest success to this first edition in the English language, and I thank ASI PUBLISHERS INC. for their collaboration.

Madras, April 1974   MICHEL BUSTROS

NOTICE TO THE FOURTH EDITION

It was in the spring of 1936 — 36 years ago now— that the first edition of this book appeared. Since then, Jupiter has completed three revolutions.

Now the reader may ask: what relation does Jupiter have to the subject of this book, the Moon and the Lunar Zodiac?

It was in the afternoon of January 20, 1936 that I delivered my manuscript to the printer (unfortunately I no longer remember the exact moment). On that day the Moon was applying to a conjunction with Jupiter in the XX Lunar Mansion, considered favorable to *writings* and to the *placing of the first stone of an edifice.*

No election chart had been calculated beforehand, and it was not until evening that I noticed, in casting the chart, that this favorable position of the two heavenly bodies was heavily afflicted by the square of Neptune. Otherwise I would have certainly chosen another day and hour, especially since the Moon was in its XXIII House, which belongs to the category of "doubtful" Houses, and does not seem to have a good influence.

Now the favorable nature of the Lunar Mansion and of the conjunction with a dignified Jupiter assured the success of this book, as demonstrated by the publication of the Argentine edition, with a preface by Boris Cristoff, completed last year (by Editorial Kier) in Buenos Aires. However, the Neptunian square and the doubtful character of the Lunar House are equally in evidence to this day. Immediately after the appearance of the first edition in June or July of 1936, the Luxembourg astrologer Ernest Hentges translated it into German; but the Nazi censor refused to authorize it, and the German edition did not see light until twenty years later in another translation! In 1939 I gave my assent to a Polish edition, which never came out because of the war. A Dutch publisher put out a very fine bound edition in 1941, under the German occupation; but I learned of its existence only twenty years later. The English translation already completed in 1970 by

Michel Bustros has been slow in coming out, etc. I have been told that there is even a clandestine version of this book in Bulgarian. . . .

The widespread acceptance of this book is not due to any achievement on my part, for there is nothing "literary" in it, but due solely to the fact that it fills an important gap in modern Astrology, since the tradition is neglected more than ever in 1972.

Whenever possible in this book, I have left out the religious and magical elements which have been grafted onto the concepts of Lunar Astrology in every country over the centuries. But it must be significant that the word for "spirits" in Burmese, *nak,* comes from the same root as *nakshatras* in the Hindu Lunar Zodiac [1]; that the genealogy of Jesus in the first chapter of the *Gospel According to Matthew* is no more than a special symbolic presentation of the lunar cycle[2]; like the twenty-eight sages or patriarchs in Buddhism from Kasyapa and his successor Ananda down to Bodhi-dharma, who assumed the direct esoteric transmission from the Buddha down to the historic founder of Chinese Zen in the seventh century; along with numerous similar occurrences.

. It is certain that the elimination of this element, prompted by the desire to emphasize the practical character of the Lunar Mansions and Houses, undeniably relegates certain interesting aspects of the question to obscurity: for example, the analogy between human destiny and a revolution of our satellite which we encounter in several religions and beliefs, most notably in the burial traditions of ancient Egypt. This analogy should be equally adaptable to precise horoscopic methods (e.g., progressions); I firmly believe that the basis of most of these beliefs — even those of non-literate peoples — derives from a civilization thoroughly impregnated with Astrology.

While on the subject of ancient Egypt, we should recall that the lunar cycle is represented there by a staircase of fourteen steps leading to a terrace on which is located "the left eye of heaven," comparable to Atoum, the Sun setting in the West. This suggests the probable correspondence of the new moon to the vernal eqiunox, and of the full moon to the autumnal, which provides a direct link between the Zodiac and the Lunar Houses. The increasing phase commands attention; the waxing of the Moon is analogous to the "filling of the eye" and its complete reconstitution. This increase, progressing from the wound made by Seth (which seems frequently to symbolize the invisible phase) to the curing of the "eye of Horus" of the full moon, is linked with the oldest myths — if we accept the testimony of several passages of texts in the pyramids.

---

*As it turns out this translation had many errors and had to be completely redone in 1974. ED.

Each phase of increase, each Lunar House symbolized by a step of the staircase equally useful for the rise toward the "fullness of the eye" as it is for the descent, is deified, as it is in many other religions including that of Greece.

"At Philae, for example, a large mural shows the king offering myrrh to fifteen deities, who promise in exchange that each will do his part to contribute to filling the eye, by means of one of the vegetable or mineral products over which he rules. (This suggests that each Lunar House was associated with a plant or mineral, astrological correspondences long since lost, but which could probably be reconstructed from archeological data with astrological verification.) The result of all this is the illumination after obscurity, the full moon after nights without moon. Among the deities in this series, we find all the primordial deities of Heliopolis, plus a few others. These same primordial deities are found again in somewhat different company in two curious interpretations, one at Edfou, the other at Dendera . . . "[3]

It must be noted that in this sanctuary, the representation appears on the south face of the pronaos, and at Dendera it is located along a staircase allowing passage to an upper terrace—which suggests, on one hand, that the staircase actually served to accomplish a ritual, for which the bas-reliefs of Edfou have recorded the theoretical image. On the other hand, it confirms our hypothesis of the correspondence between the waxing moon and the first half of the Zodiac, or rather with the feminine hemisphere; and a correspondence between the waning phase and the masculine hemisphere[4]. Since the feminine hemisphere is one of fecundity of nature, and the masculine hemisphere has a spiritual character, it is not only understandable it is profoundly logical to an astrologer that the fourteen ascending steps and fourteen descending ones of this lunar staircase in ancient Egypt are also analogous to the ages of the life of man, as well as to the sexual energy of a Bull. (The former justifies a priori all research into gressions associated with Lunar Astrology, especially since in several cosmologies—including the Babylonian—the creation of man took place at the moment of the new moon.) If the ascent of the staircase is a period of maximum fecundity and procreation, the descent is compared to the castration of the bull who becomes mere beef.

The representation of the lunation cycle by a staircase of fourteen steps equally useful for ascent and descent, may seem to be a purely Egyptian invention (or at least simply a local re-ordering of the seven planetary terraces in the Ziggurats in Mesopotamia, which face four different directions: 7 x 4 = 28, the number of the Lunar Divisions of the Zodiac and of the lunation); but the concepts are universal. In Babylon, furthermore, the day of the full moon was chosen for the ceremonies of ritual castration, as if to emphasize the idea that virility is only a function of the ascending half of the month. In the traditions of the Far East, among others, the new moon personifies the weakness and the unaware state of the infant (which was probably the original image for the characteristics of the first Lunar House); the first quarter — puberty; the full moon — the adult in full strength; the descending phase — decline and last days (XXVIII Lunar House), complete impotence and senility, corresponding to some extent to the powerlessness and sleep of the newly born.[6]

Each day had a special name in Egypt[7]. The second one was called "day of the crescent" and its equivocal and doubtful nature was emphasized by a text comparing the crescent to a knife, saying: "Is the moon not a knife? Thus she can punish the guilty."[8] Sadly, Egyptologists, as well as Assyriologists and specialists in other civilizations, are not generally interested in Astrology; I have not yet been able to find a book or article giving a complete list of these names, which would permit one to get a clear concept of the interpretation of some of these days. We know only that certain ones of the waning phase suggest a reverse reckoning.[9]

But if archeological documents of classical antiquity are precious, since they often preserve these lost elements of our own tradition, "living" data deriving from distant lands — Afghanistan, Tibet, Indonesia, the Philippines, etc., must in no way be neglected, for they can enrich our understanding.

An example:

Most European astrologers experienced real surprise in 1963 when they encountered *Le Clé de l'Astrologie Malgache* or *l'Al-Iklil* by J. Rakotonirainy[10], demonstrating the survival of an autochthonous astrological tradition in Madagascar and announcing that a Malagasy Astrological Conference took place at Tananarive from the twenty-fourth to the thirty-first of October; a preparatory meeting had been held for it a whole year before. The photo shows fifteen participants which seems to prove that it is not a case here of a few isolated astrologers as can be found in every country, but of a lively movement, one more disproof of the frequent assertion that black Africa is unaware of Astrology. Ethiopia possesses its own age-old tradition, preserved mainly in the monasteries; and astrologers are in evidence in Zanzibar and Dar-Es-Salam.

This short work began by recalling that the oldest material in French on Malagasy Astrology is found in the writings of Etienne de Flacourt who lived in Fort-Dauphin from 1648 to 1654. He describes a system used by the Anatosy who were initiated in it by the Anakara-Antenoro astrologers of Vohipeno. We can see there that the signs and divisions of the Zodiac have Arabic names — which in no way indicates a slavish copy of Arabian Astrology. After all, the greater part of the names of our stars and scientific terms (alembic, alkali, alcohol, algebra, etc.) come from the same source.

We know that *Al-Iklil* or *Iklil Al Jabbah* (The Crown of the Head) is the Arabic name of the XVII Lunar Mansion. Etienne de Flacourt points out that in Anakara Astrology the sign of Libra (or *Alimiza*) has three Houses: *Alokofora*, *Azobana* and *Alikilili* (Malagasy name for Al-Iklil). Later A. Grandidier identified Alikilili as being composed of the stars β (Graffias), δ (Isidis), and ρ of the constellation Scorpio[11], which are found today in the sign of Sagittarius. Now if we are to believe this *Clé de l'Astrology Malgache,* the Anakara astrologers, Islamized Jews who had previously emigrated to Madagascar, committed to writing in 1502 the practical use of Alikilili to determine the sighting of the Lunar Zodiac. In his communication to the Conference, Kasanga Fernand, speaking of the use of Alikilili in Malagasy astrology, states that "Alikilili is a group of stars that serve to judge and verify, as in a tribunal, the progress of the astrological calendar for the year in progress, hence the name *Adimizana* or *Balance.*"[12]

To locate the Lunar Divisions, Malagasy astrologers use a method that doesn't seem to exist elsewhere. A javelin one meter sixty centimeters in length, and a distaff sixty centimeters long, objects still in evidence in Madagascar, are placed across each other and oriented, by means of an extended arm, on the three stars of the Alikilili. The ingenuity of these astrologers in observing the heavens directly — a custom unfortunately lost in the West — is without limit; it would seem that these primitive instruments can supply the necessary correction for locating the zodiacal signs with respect to the fixed stars.

Of course we cannot follow the Malagasy in their belief in a tradition reaching all the way back to the prophet Daniel — a belief easily explained by the Jewish origins of Anakara. It should be equally surprising that a book written in *Sorabe* by Alitawarath in 1502 has not drawn the attention of the specialists and remains unknown and unpublished in Europe. Let us hope that we will be given an integral translation of it someday, and that J. Rakotonirainy or another Malagasy astrologer will publish the meanings of the Lunar and Solar Zodiac as they are in use on his island.

These remarks on the subject of ancient Egypt and Malagasy techniques show what could yet be added to this book, borrowing from archeology, ethnography and local astrological techniques. I have never claimed to have written a "definitive" or "complete" work, but only to have assembled material justifying an astrological system unjustly abandoned. Although all sciences are making rapid progress, we can state with regret that the few rare books on this subject which have come out in France in the last thirty years are only imitations of this one.

A. Volguine

January 31, 1972.
Moon in XII Lunar Mansion
and in XV Lunar House.

NOTES

[1]See Scribe, "Le monde asiatique des Esprits," in *Cahiers Astrologiques*, #155, November-December, 1971; as well as *Genies, Anges, Demons* in the collection *Sources Orientales*, vol. 8, Paris, 1971, p. 298.

[2]See A. Volguine, *Journal d'un Astrologue*, Paris, 1957, pp. 100-123.

[3]Philippe Derchain, "Mythes et dieux lunaires en Egypte" in *La Lune, Mythes et Rites*, Vol 5 of *Sources of Orientales*, Paris, 1962, p. 25.

[4]See our *Le Symbolisme de l'Aigle*, Nice, 1960, Chapter iv.

[5]Philippe Derchain, idem, pp. 27, 43.

[6]Speaking of this material and of the dating of puberty (easier to determine in women than in men; and occurring — depending on the country and the era — between 11 and 15 years with the arrival of the Moon at the exit to the VII Lunar House), we could construct a mathematically valid system of progressions in which the peak of individual development could be located equally well at thirty or at fifty years, and the decline of virility or end of female life between forty-five and seventy-eight years, since the earlier puberty arrives, the more the rhythm of progressions appears to be swift. I admit that I have made only four attempts to apply this method, which naturally belongs to the "individual measures in the horoscope." At the end of 1942, Raoul Fructus completed a book devoted to this subject, on which he had worked several years and which he hoped to publish after the war; but this work disappeared with the arrest of the author by the Gestapo. Deported to a concentration camp, he never returned. His astrological labors died with him, but the name of Raoul Fructus was given to one of the first Martinist groups after the war in Marseille.

[7]Philippe Derchain, idem, p. 29.

[8]Idem, p. 32.

[9]Idem, p.30

[10]Published by the Librairie Ny Nosy, 2 *bis* Rue Gallieni, Soarano-Antananarive, Madagascar. This House has published other astrological works, but in Malagasy.

[11]*Collections des Anciens ouvrages concernant Madagascar*, Vol VIII, p. 248.

[12]*Le Cle* . . ., p. 5.

PREFACE TO THE SECOND EDITION

The system of Lunar Astrology which is the subject of this book met with such success that within three months the first edition was practically sold out. This was especially surprising to me since Astrology publications appeal to an elite which is always a small minority.

I will not take credit for this success. It can easily be explained by the fact that everyone involved in Astrology intuitively felt the inadequacy of an exclusively solar approach. Duality is the fundamental law of the Cosmos: the temple was always supported by two pillars —*Jakim* and *Boas*. The manifestations of polarity embodied by these two pillars—one black and one white—are universal and are encountered everywhere. Sooner or later, Astrology will have to restore the Moon to its rightful place. Testing of the principles contained in this book offered results comparable to those from indications found in any modern textbook of traditional astrology. Before publishing this book, I used these principles in interpreting a large number of horoscopes so that I might judge for myself their reliability, complete them, and reject certain erroneous attributions (for example, the Hindu attribution of happiness to the Second Mansion). The letters I received after the publication of this book prove the value of this system:

"The delineations given for the Houses of the Moon are accurate" writes H.P., one of my correspondents. "On the basis of about two hundred charts that I possess, I was able to confirm the validity of these indications . . ." I take the liberty of quoting this letter, since all of the others deal with evidence from a far more limited number of cases.

Lunar Astrology should be used in every Astrological undertaking. Obviously, everything can not be applied inflexibly (this is, of course, true of any indication anywhere), but these delineations are a very important horoscopic factor; they must not be neglected in the synthesis of a horoscope.

For example, if several indications, such as Aries Ascendant plus Mars square Sun and Uranus, indicate impulsiveness and violence, whereas the Lunar Mansion indicates a gentle person — the native will of course still be impulsive, but this impulsiveness will be somewhat attenuated by the Moon. But that is the first principle of everyday Astrological synthesis.

Certain readers and even some critics of Lunar Astrology seem to confuse the invisible phase of the Moon, or *Hecate,* to which the last chapter of this book is devoted, with the hypothetical second moon called *Lilith* which appears to draw more attention from researchers every day (if one can judge by the number of articles devoted to it throughout the world). Any attentive reader will easily see that there is no relation between this hypothetical satellite and the houses of *Hecate.* I even think that in *Hecate* is localized the *dark sphere* of the occultists, the *sinister cone* of the shadow, which the earth drags after itself, and where there is an abominable reservoir whence dark forces are unleashed on our planet.

This new edition includes several improvements which make the exposition clearer and more complete. We hope that it will be received with as much interest as the first.

A.V.
Aug. 31, 1936

INTRODUCTION

There is a gap in modern Astrology, a striking inconsistency: the role assigned to the Moon.

The Sun and the Moon have visible discs of the same size. Their influence on life on our globe easily exceeds the influences of the planets, since the luminaries, as it were, regulate this life. (Are they not the basis of all calendars?) In the Astrology of the Far East, they are not part of the planetary hierarchy, because they are *Yang,* the White Dragon, the active principle, and Yin, the Black Dragon, the passive principle, which exist in each planetary element and represent the cosmic polarities (comparable to the division of humanity into two sexes).

Terrestrial life depends wholly on these two principles, since all germination, generation, development of seed and nutrition is merely the result of the reaction of a warm principle embodied in the Sun with a moist principle of the Moon. Astrologically speaking, the whole Universe exists only because of the combined action of these two principles of *Yang* and *Yin*; but we see no trace of this great law of cosmic equilibrium in the modern approach to astrology as it is practiced in Europe. That approach is profoundly Solar.

The influence of the Sun in Astrology is divided into three systems: planetary, zodiacal, and terrestrial. The twelve Houses of the horoscope and the twelve Signs of the zodiac are primarily of solar nature, since they are ultimately just the influence of the sun embodied (or reflected) in the orbit of the earth. If the signs of the zodiac were not solar by nature they would inevitably undergo constant changes in character due to the displacement of the constellations. That kind of solar influence would put the Sun on the same level as Mercury, Venus or Pluto.

And what about the Moon? Can it be reduced to the stature of a planet invisible to the naked eye such as Pluto or Mercury; although we perceive from moment to moment the Moon's astounding physical effects, such as her influence on tides and plant growth?

The Astrology of Antiquity recognized a Lunar Zodiac as well as Houses of Lunar substance, thus portioning out the influence of the Moon into three systems similar to those of Solar influence. Without this division, the place the Moon holds in the hierarchy of the planets is simply incomprehensible.

The Ancients possessed an entire Astrology based solely on the effects of the Sun and the Moon. A reasonable number of documents from every country have been passed down to us on the subject of the twenty-eight Lunar Houses and the twenty-eight Lunar Mansions, including documents from our Middle Ages. I prefer the expression *Mansions,* * taken from a manuscript of Magic[1], to more common ones such as "stations," "signs" or "courts" of the Moon, since it best translates the ancient nomenclature. In Chinese, for example, these divisions had the generic name of *siu,* and the Chinese character designating them (also pronounced *sü*), represents an inn for the night and can be translated by the verb *to rest*[2]. Our word *Mansion* comes much closer to the notion expressed by *siu* than all the other words used by various authors for this division of the Heavens into twenty-eight parts.

The antiquity of this system is incontestable, since the Indologists proved that the *nakshatras* existed in the India of the Vedic period, while the Chinese *siu* in all likelihood go back to the time of Yao, i.e., twenty-four centuries before our era. It is very probable that the Arabs got the system from the Chinese through intermediaries other than the Hindus. Lastly, the Bible knew the twenty-eight divisions as *mazzaloth* or *mazzaroth*[3], a word resembling *manzanil* of the Arabs, for which certain translations substitute *the Signs of the Zodiac,* probably for greater clarity.

"It seems likely to me," said L. de Saussure[4], "that the origin of the Lunar Zodiac common to many different peoples of Asia goes back to a prehistoric era much earlier even than the mythical reign of *Fu-Hsi* . . ."

Throughout Antiquity the importance of this division, which has been completely forgotten by modern astrologers[5], was comparable to the twelve Houses and twelve Zodiacal Signs of solar substance. The Sacred or Royal Arm of Antiquity was divided into seven palms consecrated to the seven planets and into twenty-eight fingers which were related to the twenty-eight Lunar Mansions and Houses. The twenty-eight Izeds of the Persian religion, the lunar god Soma accompanied

---

*In the French *Demeures* trans. "(Place of) residence, dwelling place, abode." ED.

by his twenty-seven wives in Hindu mythology, and the twenty-eight letters of the Arab alphabet are evident correlatives of the universally accepted twenty-eight divisions. We find this number in sociology wherever social structure is influence by astrology: for example, the twenty-eight satrapies of the Persian Empire under Cyrus[6] and the ancient feudal kingdoms of China narrowly tied to the twenty-eight *siu*. (Se-Ma Ts'ien, the greatest Chinese astrologer, says in his *Historical Memoirs*[7]: "The twenty-eight Houses preside over the twelve provces: the Dipper [Great Bear] directs them all together . . .")

It could be assumed that the number of Masters in the Masonic legend who pursued the assassins of Hiram is equally inspired by the number of Lunar Houses, since these twenty-seven Masters, successors of Hiram, can be compared to the twenty-seven wives of Soma. But the Masons have forgotten this connecttion just as the Astrologers themselves have forgotten the existence of the twenty-eight Lunar divisions.

28 is the exemplary number of life; and since the same law of analogy governs the sidereal universe and the existence of each individual, the lunar rhythm is echoed in our organism: it takes twenty-eight heartbeats for a red corpuscle to make a complete circuit of our body. Doctor Lavezzari considers *twenty-eight* the characteristic number for our circulation[8]. He says that each breath is to the circulation of the red cell as the day is to the week; while the beating of our heart, in a ratio of one to twenty-eight to the circulation of the red cell, repeats the ratio of the day to the month. Since the white cells move ten or twelve times more slowly than the red we find the ratio of the lunar month to the solar year in these two circulatory rates. The red cell must be associated with the Lunar Zodiac, while the white cell represents the Solar Zodiac in our body. It is unnecessary to insist on the symbolic import of the twenty-eight Mansions and Houses. (We must not forget that Antiquity and the Middle Ages did not dissociate the word *symbol* from the word *reality*; so they did not see in symbolism the arbitrary creations that are easily imagined in our day.) Our aim here is to make an Astrological study and to provide the practical means for using this forgotten method in day-to-day horoscopic work, and not to examine its esoteric significance. We should note only incidentally that H.A. Curtiss[9] says that the three principle grades of Initiation are presented mathematically as follows:

$$0+1+2+3+4=10$$ Cycle of Nature or of physical conditions, whose symbol is the scepter.

(10) +5 +6 +7 =28 =10	Cycle of man or of the Christic force, whose symbol is the cloak or the priestly vestment.
(28) +8 +9 +10 =55 =10	Cycle of the Superman or Higher Self, whose symbol is the lighted taper or the lantern of Hermes.

Thus, esoterically, the lunar cycle of twenty-eight Mansions and Houses is located between the primitive natural Zodiac of ten signs (whose traces are found in every tradition) and Divinity.

The twenty-eight Mansions are fixed, beginning with $0°$ Aries and superimposed, as it were, on the twelve signs of the Zodiac. They are much less complex than the Houses, just as the Solar Signs are more easy to examine than the twelve Houses of the horoscope.

In ancient China this Lunar Zodiac played a more important role than the Solar Zodiac. It must never be forgotten that the Chinese system is profoundly original and that it was formed in deepest antiquity, about twenty-five centuries B.C., independently of the Babylonian system (which is ours). The ancient Chinese linked their Solar Zodiac with the planet Jupiter who circles the heavens in twelve years, and the Lunar Zodiac with Saturn whose revolution takes twenty-eight years. Jupiter is more extroverted, more material than the pale star of Chronos; so we may assume that the Lunar Zodiac is more esoteric and more introverted than the Solar Zodiac[10]. This explains, for example, why the Zodiac, or more frequently the number twenty-eight, is often associated with initiation and the invisible world. The Annamese believed, for example, that the normal time between two incarnations was twenty-eight months.

Hindu Astrology — which seems to us much less original than is generally claimed, since it is nothing more than a combination of the Babylonian and the Chinese systems — believes that in intrauterine existence, the individual develops around two force centers or *chakras,* the first of which — *Pingala* — is the cardiac Lotus of twelve petals, a type of microcosmic transposition of the Solar Zodiac; while the second — the Lunar *Ida* — is none other than the human center of the twenty-eight Mansion Zodiac. Just as the Sun and the Moon form the two eyes of *Vaivasvata* in the planetary system and the two Zodiacs, Solar and Lunar, perpetuate the same principle in the Zodiacal system, similarly *Pingala* and *Ida* are the force centers of the development of the human foetus — future microcosm.

In ancient Egypt the Lunar Zodiac symbolized by Osiris who was said to have lived, or rather reigned, twenty-eight years[11]; whose body was torn into fourteen pieces (number of houses of the Moon increasing or decreasing); and whom Typhon began to dismember at the time of the Full Moon. (This foreshadows the Moon losing a piece of herself on each of the fourteen days which make up the second half of the lunar month.)

It is unnecessary to continue these remarks, which show clearly that all traditions agree in assigning great importance to the Lunar system, almost always the same importance as to the Solar system — the only one we use today.

NOTES

[1]Picatrix,"La Clef des Clavicules," 1256, manuscript of the Bibliotéque de l'Arsenal. P. Piobb reproduced several passages of this manuscript in his *Formulaire de la Haute Magie.*

[2]cf. "Zeitrechnung der Chinesen," cited by L. Saussure, *Les Origines de l'Astronomie Chinoise,* p. 46.

[3]The Second Book of Kings, XXIII, 5; Book of Job, XXXVIII, 32.

[4]*The Origins of Chinese Astrology,* p. 281.

[5]In all of French astrological literature, only the course of F. Rolt-Wheeler mentions this division (sixty-sixth lesson), but he calls the Mansions, "Houses"—which only increases the confusion that reigns in this area.

[6]See my essay on Astrology in Persia in *L'Astrosophie,* issue of August, 1935.

[7]T. III, p. 405, ttranslated by E. Chavannes, Paris 1895.

[8]"Rythmes Humains, Rythmes Cosmiques," in *Astrosophie,* April, 1936, p. 183.

[9]"The Key to the Universe," p. 307. It is one of the basic works of *The Order of Christian Mystics.*

[10]We should observe that Occidental Astrology attributes the North Node of the Moon's orbit to Jupiter and the South Node to Saturn, and this attribution can be thought of as parallel to the connection of the Zodiacs to these two planets in the tradition of the Far East.

[11]Plutarch, *Isis and Osiris,* 13.

THE INTERPRETATIONS
OF THE TWENTY-EIGHT MANSIONS
IN DIFFERENT TRADITIONS

The simultaneous evolution of Astrology in different countries has given rise to very evident differences in viewpoint which frequently mislead researchers. But this phenomenon is encountered in the field of every science. In medicine, for example, we find not only very different systems—almost opposed, such as the occidental and the Chinese system, but even very noticeable differences between modern French medicine and German medicine, and the simultaneous existence in each country of two systems: allopathy and homeopathy.

So it will not be surprising that the boundaries of the Lunar Mansions are not always the same in every tradition. The Arabic and Occidental tradition (which we follow here) differ noticeably from certain documents (probably altered), which not only give other boundaries, but even change the number of the Mansions, which they put at twenty-seven or twenty-nine instead of twenty-eight.

It is very likely that considerations of an extra-astrological order played a great role in the determination of the number of Mansions. Such is the opinion of Pierre Orletz, for example, who writes:

"My friend, the astrologer, A. Volguine tells me that the revolution of the Moon was calculated differently by different peoples, and that besides the generally accepted number of twenty-eight days, in certain parts of India and sometimes in ancient Egypt the Lunar Houses numbered twenty-seven, while among certain Arab and Touareg tribes they numbered twenty-nine.

"The sidereal revolution of the Moon in relation to the Zodiac takes twenty-seven days, seven hours, forty-three minutes; and the synodic revolution in relation to the Sun takes twenty-nine days, twelve hours, forty-four minutes.

"I assumed that perhaps it was a matter of symbolism: some being inclined to the idea of 3x3x3, others to 7x4, and those who chose twenty-nine had all my sympathies. I attach particular importance to this last number: circumference divided by diameter gives 3.1415 . . . or approximately 22/7 where 22 represents the circumference and 7, the diameter. The sum $22+7=29$ suggests a concept of totality, of the unity of the containing and the contained, of the exterior and interior, of the principle and the manifestation . . ."[1]

This opinion of Pierre Orletz enlarges upon that of L.C. de Saint-Martin who devotes #XXII of "Numbers" to this question, under the heading "Phases of the Moon." This paragraph says:

"3x9 =27, terrestrial factors and products. This is the Moon's limit on the surface of our planet.

"4x7 =28, celestial factors and products. Actually the four phases depend on the aspect from the Sun. But from here we cannot see the twenty-eighth day of the Moon, because the quaternary and the decenary do not belong to the material Earth. They are manifested to us spiritually, and they are imperceptible on the material plane. The Sun has its noontide, the Moon must have hers; but what comparison of these two noontides . . ."[2]

Whatever the bases for the different systems of the Lunar Zodiac, we cannot ignore them, especially the Chinese system with its very unequal Mansions; the diagram for this system is on the following page and the following chapter is devoted to it. But we prefer to recommend the regular divisions whose traces are found in all traditions, even in the Chinese tradition.

These divisions should "color" each horoscopic factor located therein, but here we will study only the indications offered by the Moon in its movement around the Zodiac, lest we further complicate the description of this method, which is complementary to the solar method — the only one used by the Western astrologers today.

The interpretations of the position of the Moon in each of these twenty-eight Mansions may be summarized in the following manner:

MANSION I, from $0°$ $0'$ to $12°$ $51'$ $26''$ Aries. —called *Almach* in the Occidental tradition, a name borrowed from the star in the left foot of the constellation Andromeda[3]. It signifies an ardent imagination, taste for occult sciences, and many changes in employment throughout life. Picatrix advises that the transit of the Moon through this Mansion be used to make pentacles for journeys and for working of spells for love and hatred.

LE SYSTÈME CHINOIS DES DIVISIONS INÉGALES

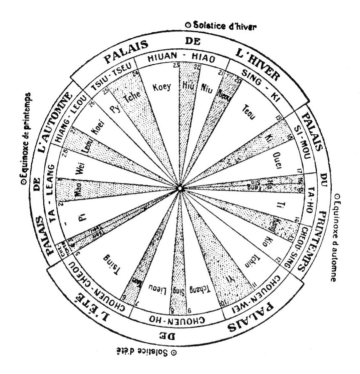

This diagram represents the division of the equator into twenty-eight *siu* twenty-four hundred years B.C., the result of the reconstruction of the ancient Lunar "Zodiac" of the Chinese by L. de Saussure.

This representation should be considered approximate and not as ex- act in all details, for Biot thinks that before the XII century B.C. China recognized only twenty-four sieou, and that the VII,XIV,XXI, and XXVIII divisions were introduced by the duke of Chiu the great reformer of Chinese Astrology.

This plate was taken from: *The Origins of Chinese Astronomy*.

The Hindus called the Mansion *Asvini,* the *Horsemen,* because it appeared to confer a great need for movement. They considered this *nakshatra* (Indian word for *Mansion*) an indication of personal charm, elegance, love of jewelry, and popularity. It also facilitates comprehension.

Known among the Arabs by the name *Al Sharatain,* (which is derived from the name of the star on the north horn of the constellation Aries — *Sharatan,* just as the West named this Mansion after one of the principle stars in the constellation Andromeda). It symbolizes forces in conflict, whirlwinds, which are expressed in day-to-day life by quarrels. The Arabs state that this Mansion exerts a very favorable influence on business.

The Chinese gave it the name of *Mao* (Pleiades), and interpret it as the mark of a career filled with many salient events, and in no way a flat level existence. Statistics could easily show the validity of this statement, but the charts I have seem to confirm it in a striking manner. I found the Moon occupying this Mansion in several far from ordinary destinies, beginning with those of General de Gaulle and the last Czar, Nicholas II, and ending with that of a victim of the desert whose horoscope was published in #II of "Grand Nostradamus."

We should observe that the importance of this *siu* is underscored by the fact that Chinese astrologers called the *Root of the Heavens* and the *Commander of the Asterisms.*

The Kabbalists know the First Mansion as *Aiah** which means the train of a sacerdotal robe. They regarded this Mansion as a mark of authority.

Obviously, the solar House where this Mansion falls in each particular case, offers the possibility of greater precision and development of these interpretations. If it is found in the Second solar House, the native will obtain authority by his work; in the Third solar House, he will have authority over his brothers, sisters, and cousins; in the Fourth, his parents will be more or less subject to his influence, or this authority will be manifested in his home, or, again, he will obtain his authority toward the end of his days; in the Fifth, the native will be authoritative in love, and if his partner were not sufficiently docile to his whims, he would seek another partner and could become inconstant and flighty, passing from one mistress to another, driven by the unconscious need to demonstrate his authority; in the Sixth, the native will obtain this authority by active and energetic occupations; in

---

*These designations are not translations of the Hebrew. The Hebrew is an alphabetical acrostic of the combinations of each succeeding letter of the Hebrew alphabet (22 letters + 5 final forms) with the suffix of God's name "iah" attached. ED.

the Seventh, the authority will be exercised in marriage — which doesn't promise much happiness, etc.

In any case, the statements of different traditions which we have summarized, already allow us to add many indications to ordinary interpretation each time that the Moon in a nativity is between $0°$ and $12°$ 51' 26" Aries.

Lastly, we should emphasize that all traditions are in perfect agreement on the principle of this Mansion, although they express it differently. Behind *the fiery imagination* of the occidental tradition, the *need for movement* of the Hindus, the *whirlwinds* of the Arabs, the *eventful destiny* of the Chinese, etc., we clearly feel the same dynamic force which each one expresses differently, but which possesses its individual characteristics not found in any other Mansion.

MANSION II, from $12°$ 51' 27" to $25°$ 42' 52" Aries. — called *Albothaïm* by Picatrix who advises that the transit of the Moon through this Mansion be used to work spells of enmity and to make pentacles for the discovery of springs and treasures. (In other words, this Mansion seems to give aptitude for radiesthesia)[5]. It gives courage, but also recklessness and indicates the will and energy to direct one's own life by ambition or by thought and not by feelings. Lastly, according to Cardan, the position of the Moon in this Mansion gives only inconstant and variable wealth.

We should mention that Agrippa[6] uses names for the Mansions other than those we give in the course of this summary; but these names seem to be distortions of those of Picatrix. Thus for example, Agrippa called the First Mansion *Alnath* instead of *Almach,* the second *Allothaïm* or *Albochan* instead of Albothaïm, etc.

To this mansion, called *Bharani,* the *Bearer,* the Hindus attributed luck in life, maternal love, triumph over illness[7] and determination in work.

Among the Hebrews, it was called *Biah* which designates the *Path of Wisdom.* It promises the achievement of wisdom after much effort and frequently varied tasks, moments of recklessness caused by lack of reflection and of life experience. The charts of H.C. Agrippa, author of *La Philosophie Occulte,* of Booker John and of many others seem to confirm this promise of wisdom.

Called *Al Butani,* the *Belly of the Celestial Ram* by the Arabs, this Mansion is considered unfavorable for sea journeys. (My own observations seem to show that sea voyages of people having the Moon in this part of the heavens, are always tied to painful events such as death, exile, or bad business dealings; or when it is a case of cruises or travel for pleasure, they take place under unfavorable conditions, for example, a tempest during the crossing.) The Arabs attribute to this Mansion favorable influence on trade and the discovery of treasures.

In the Chinese system, this Mansion *Pi* or the *Snare* creates the danger of rash actions which like the net or the trap paralyze the freedom of the subject. The reckless love affairs of Henry IV who had the Moon in $21°$ Aries or the political involvements undertaken thoughtlessly by the assassinated dictator of Louisiana Huey P. Long, whose Moon was in $15°$ 29' Aries, allow us to grasp the idea that Chinese astrologers wanted to embody in the *Snare*. Leon Degrelle, the leader of the Belgian *rexists* also had the Moon in this section of the heavens ($17°$ 3' Aries), which could have given warning of frequent recklessness in his political actions.

We must remember that when the Moon in this second Mansion falls in the Second, Fifth, Seventh, or Eighth solar House in masculine charts, it seems to indicate an extravagant and flirtatious woman; in the Fifth solar House, it also is the sign of inconstancy in love; in the Eleventh House, a sign of the protection of a married woman or widow, etc.

MANSION III, from $25°$ 42' 53" Aries to $8°$ 34' 18" Taurus. — called *Ascorija* by Picatrix, the doctor and astrologer of Arab origin who initiated Alphonse X, king of Castille, and consequently one of the founders of the Astrology of Occidental Europe. He advises that the transit of the Moon through this Mansion be used for alchemical experiments, for working spells of love and making pentacles for sea journeys. Its influence seems to accentuate the power of feelings and determination, and to confer a great capacity for work. The charts of George Sand whose Moon was in $26°$ 40' Aries, Adrien Marquet (Moon in Taurus $6°$ 13'), Dr. Hjalmar Schacht (Moon in Taurus $6°$ 25') and many others confirm this attribution.

Arabic *Al Thuraya,* the *Swarm*: this Mansion is considered favorable for the sciences and for all who live outdoors, but unfavorable for marriage or travel by water. It increases the practical instinct and seems to be especially related to sciences demanding the use of this ability, for example economics, accounting, etc. It is not accidental that M. Wemyss attributes geography to $26°$ Aries; teaching to $28°$; la différenciation to $29°$; mathematics to $2°$ Taurus; strategy to $3°$; diplomacy to $5°$, etc. Behind all these specific attributions, the concept of the practical sciences emerges.

In India this Mansion is known as *Krittika,* the *Celestial Commander,* which is the Hindu name for the Pleiades. It makes one very susceptible to women (which almost always leads to adultery and complicated affairs of the heart), but indicates at the same time a good reputation and a good personality.

In the Hindu system, *Krittikas, the Pleiades* are the spouses of the Seven Rishis (Great Bear) and the nurses to Kartikeya, God of War who can be identified with Mars or Saint Michael[7]. Since Krittikas presides over the dark age *Kali-Yuga,* the age of sin and sorrows, the *nakshatra* which bears this name always causes some ups and downs in the private life (generally corresponding to the solar House where this Mansion is located).

We should mention that in India Krittikas begins the Lunar Zodiac just as Mao begins it in China. In the stellar symbolism of most peoples the Pleiades occupy a central place; the reasons for this escape us today, but perhaps they would be in agreement with the opinion put forth by certain astronomers, that the Pleiades, particularly *Alcyone,* are the center of our universe. The Babylonians called Alcyone *Temennu, the Foundation Stone;* the Arabs, *Kimah,* which means the *Immortal Seal,* and *Al Wasat,* the Center or the Middle. The Hindus called Alcyone *Amba, the Mother* which could be interpreted in the sense of Mother of the Lunar Zodiac.

It is also the siu *Tse* (Head of Orion) in the Far East. The Chinese astrologers attribute to it independence of thought which may provoke some debates and even quarrels with significant results during the life of the native.

The Hebrews call this Mansion *Giah, He Who Repays,* and say that Fate, good or evil, is always powerful with persons having the Moon in this Mansion. In spite of their abilities and their capacity for work, free will seems to play a small part in their life.

I should add that very often the Hindu or Chinese attributions repeat some Arab signification or other. To avoid useless repetition, I mention a signification only once if it is common to all traditions, putting it ahead of the significations peculiar to each civilization. For example, I placed at the head of the list devoted to this Mansion: *powerful emotions, determination,* and *great capacity for work.*

MANSION IV, from 8° 34' 19" to 21° 25' 44" Taurus. — In the Middle Ages, it had the name of Aldebaran, the star of the eye of the constellation Taurus and one of the royal stars of antiquity. Picatrix recommends that the transit of the Moon through this Mansion be used for working spells of enmity of all kinds. Although charts of people connected with spells are very difficult to find, my collection of horoscopes confirms the "magic" nature of this Mansion. The reader will find one of these charts later in the chapter devoted to *Lunar Houses*.

In the natal chart, this Mansion signifies a great deal of diplomacy and predicts violent feelings and irresistible passions under the appearance of good nature, especially if the native is sensual.

The Arab astrologers called this Mansion by the same name as the Christian writers of the Middle Ages did: *Al-Debaran, the Eye of God*[8]. They interpreted this *manazil* as a favorable sign for work, manufacture and small trade; but unfavorable for real estate, building, and everything having to do with mines. It is also the sign of marriage, but at the same time one of discord in the conjugal or natal home.

Known in India as *Rohini*, the *Red Stag*, this Mansion is considered the sign of mental stability and of kindness. According to the Hindu astrologers, a man having the Moon in this section of the heavens often imperceptibly but surely achieves the power of eluding obstacles, but is capable of showing some vulgarity or chicanery.

Symbolized in the Kabbalistic system as *Diaih, the Gate of the Light*, it indicates that obstacles in life must be surmounted by the energy of the native.

Among the Chinese it is the *siu Tsan* or *the Heart of the Warrior Tsan*, (Orion) bearing the name of the same constellation as the preceding Mansion — which encouraged certain writers to combine these two *siu*. Its interpretation is about the same as that of the preceding *siu*, although Tsan is considered more favorable than Tse. This Mansion, according to Chinese astrologers creates the danger of some hardships at the beginning of life and exposes the native to being himself the direct cause of quarrels or regrettable vexations.

MANSION V, from 21° 25' 45" Taurus to 4° 17'10" Gemini. — In the Grimoires of Magic of the Middle Ages it bears several names whose etymological origin is difficult to establish: *Aluxer, Abnicoiz*, and *Alingez*. The transit of the Moon through this Mansion was considered favorable to the development of talents and aptitudes, since it signifies a well endowed and artistic nature. "La Clef des Clavicules" advises that the Moon's residence in this section of the heavens be used for working spells for and against friendship and to prepare pentacles for travel, since its influence is clearly favorable for travel and change of residence.

Agrippa, who named this Mansion *Alshataia* or *Albashaia*, says that it gives health and benevolence.

Called *El Hakah, the White Spot* by the Arabs, this Mansion is considered favorable to studies and the second half of journeys. According to Arabs, the Moon in this *manazil* nevertheless exerts an unfavorable influence on associations, collective enterprises, and on charitable and humanitarian works, being more propitious for private life than for social activity.

The Hindus state that this *nakshatra* which they call *Mrigasiras* causes shyness in the beginning of life and denotes a clever and persuasive man, but at the same time sensual and fickle.

Called *Tsing, the Well* by the astrologers of the Far East, this Mansion favors slow and laborious accumulation of wealth and exerts a favorable influence on poets. We should mention that the charts of F. Mistral, Alexandre Dumas senior, of Paul Valéry, of C. Mendes and many others have the Moon in that Mansion.

Lastly, the Hebrews called it *Eiah, the Supreme,* and attributed to it a good influence on education.

MANSION VI, from 4° 17' 11' to 17° 8' 36" Gemini. — called *Athaia* or *Alkaia* by Picatrix. It is the sign of a providential protection throughout life, and Picatrix's advice to use the transit of the Moon in this Mansion for working spells destined to give victory in war, reflects the idea of a providence connected with this part of the heavens.

Manazil Al Hanach, the Scar of the Arab astrologers. This Mansion is believed to exert an unfavorable influence on farm work, — which explains the statement of the *Clef des Clavicules* that it favors working of spells to curse crops. This *Manazil* further signifies some financial losses in the course of life and slows convalescences.

Kew, the Ghost of the Chinese. This siu, contrariwise, is considered very favorable for business in the Far-Eastern system. It also seems to have a conncetion with social and political life. (Mussolini's chart, who has the Moon at 9° 46' Gemini, or Paul Reynaud's[9] with the Moon at 8° 37' Gemini — is it a coincidence?). But it is interesting to observe that the Chinese tradition agrees with the Arab tradition in recognizing the devitalizing character of this Mansion. Where the Arabs believe it slows recovery after illnesses, the Chinese say that it is one of the indicators of a short life.

Known to the Hindus as *Ardra, Moisture,* it indicates pride deriving from consciousness of worth, a certain malice, little gratitude, and it seems to give a tendency to treachery, and deceptions concerning business or finance.

Viah for the Kabbalists, this Mansion indicates proselytising and can be used for all kinds of foundations.

MANSION VII, from 17° 8' 37" Gemini to 0° Cancer. — In Picatrix it is referred to by three names *Addyvat, Aldyaras* and *Aldry-abe* which are simple derivations of the Arabic *Aldhira.* It is the Mansion of scholars; its influence is exercised especially on the mental and intuitive plane. The charts of Regiomontanus, Pasteur, C.A. Calmette, P. Choisnard and many others seem to confirm this aspect of *Addyvat.*

Picatrix recommends using the transit of the Moon through this Mansion to prepare pentacles intended to promote trade, sea voyages and luck in general, as well as to work spells to obtain the favor of great ones and to sow discord.

The Arabs call it *Al Dhira, the Seed* or *the Branch*; they consider it favorable for lovers, friendships, earnings, and for healing; but unfavorable for Law and Justice.

The Hindus knew this Seventh Mansion[10] as *Punarvasu, Brothers returned.* They attribute to it an amiable, understanding and reasonable character, capable of being happy with little. Its influence is opposed to worldly life and inclines the native to a life more or less retired from the world, living in the intimacy of family or with some friends. Love of travel and great attachment to the home make the person with this position of the Moon one who adores traveling and hates to move.

My personal observations permit me to add that very often it is the work and the occupation of the native that force him to lead such a retired life.

In China it is the *siu Liu, a Willow Branch*. There this Mansion is associated with the ancestor cult and is considered favorable to family life although it causes considerable changes in life style in youth.

Ziah for the Kabbalists, this Mansion develops trust and promotes friendship.

In concluding the First quarter of the Lunar Zodiac, we should say that, like the signs, the decans, the terms, and the degrees, each of these Mansions is linked to a planet, in the occidental tradition as well as in Hindu astrology. We will devote a separate chapter to the latter since its attributions do not agree with ours. In the Western tradition the First Mansion Mansion is governed by the Sun; the Second by the Moon; the Third by Mars; the Fourth by Mercury; the Fifth by Jupiter; the Sixth by Venus; and the Seventh by Saturn; the order of rulership is the same as that of the week.

The three remaining quarters of the Lunar Zodiac repeat this order of planetary rulerships.

MANSION VIII, from 0° to 12° 51' 26" Cancer. — *Amathura* or *Alamiathra*. Its influence is especially favorable as regards the family since it gives a profound attachment to the family and love of children (even those of a stranger). Picatrix advises that the transit of the Moon through this Mansion be used to prepare the pentacles for love and friendship and for land travel as well as to work spells of friendship and enmity "against captives or to bind someone in captivity."

Al Nathrah, the Nursery of the Arabs, makes the native somewhat credulous, but promises that love or friendship will begin in the course of travel.

Hsing to the Chinese, this Mansion is interpreted in the Celestial Empire as the sign of charity and of the need to dedicate and even sacrifice oneself for dear ones or for ideas. The chart of Miss Lind-af-Hageby[11], who dedicated her life to works of charity and to the protection of children and animals, has the Moon at 4° 22' Cancer; we should ask if it is possible to explain this chart completely without taking this Mansion into consideration. Especially since these philanthropic tendencies are found in *all* persons having the Moon in this Mansion, even Hugo Stimnes[12] and F.D. Roosevelt, while the dedication to a noble cause marks charts as varied as that of Dr. Benes[13], Theophile Delcassé and Emile Loubet.

Called *Pushya, the Flower* by the Hindus, it is believed to promote renown and popularity and to indicate a thrifty virtuous and peaceful person. It is also the sign of tenacity in action, of will power set on a chosen goal, and of the difficulty of stopping the native when he chooses a false path or takes a wrong direction. (like Dr. Petiot whose Moon is in Cancer 6° 43')[14].

MANSION IX, from 12° 51' 27" to 25° 42'52" Cancer. — In Picatrix it bears the name *Atars* or *Atarls;* he advises it be used to make magic pentacles intended to curse journeys and sow discord, as well as for spells for hatred. At the moment of birth, it imparts a sort of romanticism that has a marked effect on actions, which we find in Gambetta, Ed. Herriot, A. Besant and many others whose Moon is in this Mansion.

Al Tarf, the Gaze of the Arabs; it marks one affable and benevolent, but acts in various ways depending on sex: in a masculine chart it favors marriage and increases the force of personality; in a feminine horoscope, it exercises a bad influence on marriage and makes the native easily discouraged, sullen and unhappy.

Obviously, if the Moon is afflicted, it cannot exercise a good influence on the marriage of the man, especially since it is the principal significator of the wife in a masculine chart.

Called *Chang, the Bended Bow* by the Chinese, it signifies prudence, tenacity, and stability. According to the astrologers of the Far-East, a journey should not be begun when the Moon is in this *siu*, because it exerts a bad influence on travel.

Known to the Hindus by the name of *Aslesha, the Web,* this *nakshatra* predisposes the native to lack of sincerity, avarice and to numerous deceptions and disappointments. This division of the Lunar Zodiac encourages elevation of the mind to a synthetical vision of things but at the same time provokes painful separations in life or serious troubles due to familial, emotional, commercial, social or political disunity.

Tiah, the Sense of Beauty, to the Kabbalists. This Mansion imparts a great need of faith (which does not seem to always mean religious faith), and desire for authority, but doesn't indicate a sense of responsibility.

MANSION X, from 25° 42' 53" Cancer to 8° 34' 18" of Leo. — Known in Europe as *Alzezal, Algelhab* or *Algelba.* It indicates a mixture of kindness and calculation *"La Clef des Clavicules"* recommends that the transit of the Moon through this Mansion be used to make pentacles for love and to work spells intended to dispose of enemies, strengthen buildings and procure benevolence and aid.

Al Jabbah, Forehead of the Lion, to the Arabs. This Mansion is considered very favorable from all aspects, for studies as well as for earnings, for professional success as well as for love; but often makes the native very sensitive to the feelings of others and inclines him to abuse of drugs and medications.

I (Wing) to the Chinese, this Mansion is also considered a favorable factor in social elevation, particularly where due to the native's own efforts.

Magha, the Mighty of the Hindus, indicates in India an industrious, religious man, possessing a great deal of tact and having many opportunities to achieve wealth, but experiencing restlessness in life, often as a result of personal ambitions.

Iiah, the Absolute Principle of the Kabbalists, indicates a broad field of activity and is believed to exert a favorable influence from a spiritual aspect (which must have something to do with the fact that this Mansion is considered by the Hebrews the center of the Lunar Zodiac).

MANSION XI, from 8° 34' 19" to 21° 25' 44" Leo.—Called *Azobre*, according to Picatrix who associates it with pentacles intended to favor trade and with spells to enable prisoners to escape and for laying siege to fortresses. It gives persons under its influence idealism or very refined tastes, but indicates vacillating fortune. We find the Moon in this Mansion with Mahatma Gandhi, Leopold III, king of Belgium, G. Madel, General Weygand, etc.

Al Zubrah, the Mane of the Celestial Lion of the Arabs. This Mansion exerts a favorable influence on trade, on wealth (which often comes as a result of the efforts of others, especially in charts of women), on marriage and travel, but it is considered an unfavorable influence for the health of women.

Chin, Servitude of the Chinese, this *siu* symbolizes patient courage and susceptibility but cautions the native to choose his words carefully and beware outbursts of anger.

Called *Purva Phalguni, the Front of the Culprit* by the Hindus. This Mansion indicates eloquence or facility with words, love of travel, and pride or vanity; but threatens accidents by fire (this seems particularly true when the Moon is Hyleg or occupies the VI or VII solar House).

Kiah, the Unchangeable of the Kabbalists. This section of the heavens is considered favorable to all premeditated action with a clearly determined goal; but unfavorable for risk.

MANSION XII, from 21° 25' 45" Leo to 4° 17' 10" Virgo.—Called *Atorsiana* or *Discorda* by the astrologers of Medieval Europe. In certain lists of significations for the Lunar Zodiac it is associated with the invisible world on the one hand, and social (even socialist) ideas on the other; the charts of Marconi, who dedicated his life to the study of waves and whose Moon is in Leo 25° 47'; and Sepharial (Moon in Leo 22° 45') seem to confirm the connection this Mansion has with the invisible world, while the horoscopes of Upton Sinclair (Moon in Leo 27° 56'), Josef Stalin (whose Moon is 3° 22' Virgo) and even that of Soviet Russia[15] corroborate the second signification of this Mansion.

Picatrix advises that the transit of the Moon through this Mansion be used to make pentacles favorable to crops, and to work spells intended to improve the lot of prisoners, slaves and friends, as well as to destroy ships.

The Arabs call this *manazil Al Sarfah, the Changer of Weather,* and consider it favorable to agriculture, the sending of messages, and for those who work for others as employees or salaried personnel. It seems that this Mansion should be placed among the factors favoring elevation in life in the service of another.

Chinese: *Chio, the Horns of the Dragon.* This Mansion plays a very large part in the astrology of the Far-East. Schlegel calls it the *Patriarch of the Constellations,* while Lide Saussure, designates it as the *Foremost of the Signs.* It is less favorable for women than for men; to the latter it gives wisdom and promises success in life as well as a happy and advantageous marriage; in feminine charts, according to the Chinese, it inclines the native to virginity or celibacy, or perhaps to diseases of the uterus and to emotional deceptions.

In the Hindu Zodiac it is *Uttara Phalguni, the Back of the Culprit.* A joyous and happy influence is attributed to it, but it is very possible that this attribution derives more from the location of this *nakshatra* than from astrological observations: according to the Ginzel, the oldest texts show the festival of spring associated with the Full Moon in *Phalguni.* In China as well, the Full Moon which appeared to the left of the signal star of the *Kio* was the First in the year; the apparition of the Horns of the Dragon at twilight was the sign of the new year. Be that as it may, the Hindus state that this Mansion denotes love and sensuality, happiness and knowledge as well as wealth acquired through personal merit. Statistics and observations will allow us to determine how much truth there is in these assertions.

We should add that the Hindus frequently combine the Eleventh and Twelfth House, since the Moon in this section of the heavens emphasizes sensuality and makes of this trait a strong influence on the career (as also of the sexual life in general and amorous adventures in particular), making a union (or unions) the decisive factor of social success or, contrarily, the direct cause of the loss of position, and occasionally even a real catastrophe destroying with a single stroke a whole existence. (This depends on aspects received and the whole of the chart).

Liah, the Paths of Wisdom to the Hebrews. This Mansion is believed to encourage study but to bring at the same time too much versatility.

MANSION XIII, from 4° 17' 11' to 17° 8' 36" Virgo. — Called *Alalma, Asalame* and *Alhahuhe* by Picatrix[16]. He recommends that the Lunar transit through this House be used to make the pentacles intended to promote trade and crops, and to work spells for the escape of prisoners and to gain the good will of the mighty. In natal charts it indicates cleverness in the handling of money or in other words increases financial skill. The charts of John Pierpont Morgan, (who has the Moon ino Virgo 14°), Camille Chautemps (whose Moon is at 10° 24' of the same sign), and others confirm this indication.

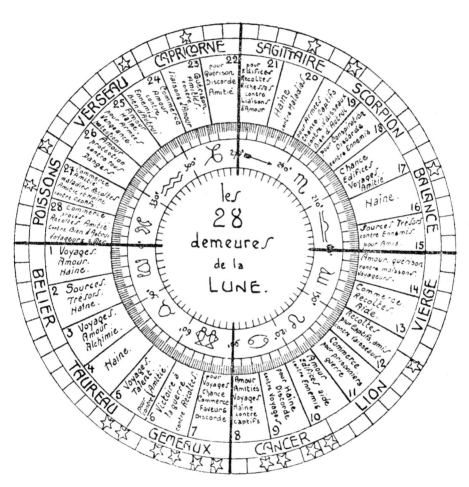

THE LUNAR ZODIAC

The significations inscribed in the circle summarize the data from Picatrix, Arab astrologer and doctor, who lived in Spain in the XIII Century, and whose works were translated into Spanish around 1256, by order of Alphonse X, king of Castille.

(This plate is taken from *Secrets, #26.*)

It is even possible that this peculiarity of the thirteenth Mansion extends a little beyond its limits. A. Stavisky[17], for example, had the Moon in Virgo 19° 42' which is 2° 5' outside of this Mansion. In any case, whenever the Moon is found at the boundary of two Mansions, I advise astrologers to take the interpretations of both Mansions (just as you do for a planet in the twenty-ninth degree of a sign).

Known to the Arabs by the name of *Al Awwa, the Barking Dog,* this Mansion is considered a sign of discernment, benevolence, even of a certain methodical kindness which may, however, be hidden under a gruff exterior. It is considered a good influence on travel, but they state that the profit derived therefrom generally passes into other hands.

Chinese *Kang, the Other Horn of the Dragon Ch'en*: This Mansion is, conversely, regarded in an unfavorable light, according to the statements of the astrologers of the Far-East. This *siu* always provokes several unfavorable events in the course of the life of the native completely independent of his will, but influencing his life strikingly. Very often these events are of a collective nature—floods, wars, revolutions, etc. In the horoscopes of sensual persons, this *siu* indicates that they are slaves to their own desires. From the standpoint of health, the Moon in this Mansion demands particular care with food and avoidance of all excessive eating.

In India it is *Hasta, the Hand, nakshatra* of the industrious man, inventive and subtle, who frequently possesses an elastic conscience. It is the image of daily work and achievement in performing an undertaking (e.g. as an artisan), rather than leadership. When the Moon occupies this Mansion in a horoscope the question of morality must be given careful attention.

The Kabbalists call it *Miah, Secret Things*; they attribute to it a good influence in good charts, and an unfavorable influence in afflicted charts (which reconciles the Chinese and the Arab points of view). In an afflicted horoscope it denotes secrets in the life of the native.

MANSION XIV, from 17° 8' 37" Virgo to 0° Libra.—It is *Achmech, Azimel* or *Azimech* in the "Clef des Clavicules," which advises that the transit of the Moon through this part of the heavens be used to make pentacles for love and for healing of the sick. This Lunar transit, according to Picatrix, also exerts a propitious influence on spells intended to destroy harvests and plants; to harm travelers or bless navigation, as well as for spells to bring happiness to heads of state and their friends.

In horoscopes, it increases prudence and the ability to analyze, and at the same time seems to promote divinatory studies and experiments (clairvoyance, tarot, etc.).

Al Simac, the Unarmed Man for the Arab astrologers. This Mansion does not seem to favor journeys. It also exerts an unfavorable influence on the first years of marriage, but the causes of dissension seem to disappear later; or if the marriage was made without love, sincere and deep affection comes with age.

Chinese *Ti, the Roof*. This *siu* seems to favor responsibility, serious thought, and the rise to a responsible station nevertheless dependent on others. The emperor of Japan with the Moon at 22° 30' Virgo and Pope Pius XI whose Moon is in 18° 24' of the same sign — are they really autocrats? It is more than doubtful. Even around Colonel de la Rocque whose Moon is at 17° 44' Virgo, influences can be imagined which noticeably diminish his personal power. This last example belongs to the XXIII and not to the XIV Mansion.

In India this Mansion is known by the name of *Chitra, the Light*. We should mention that it has given its name to the month *Caïtra*, which embraces this Mansion and the next, just as *Magha* and *Phalguni* gave their names to the preceding months; and that Hindu astrologers attribute more importance to the *nakshatra* that give their names to months than to any others. They attribute to *Chitra* elegance and personal charm, an intuitive but often indecisive mind (since the native likes to weigh the pros and the cons), and lack of courage.

Niah, the Gates of the Light of the Hebrews. This Mansion is believed to favor wisdom in old age, and makes persons born under its influence very respected and listened to in their last years.

This Mansion ends the second septenary of the Lunar Zodiac.

MANSION XV, from 0° to 12° 51' 26" Libra. — It is called *Algaphia* and *Algalia* by Picatrix who recommends that the transit of the Moon through this Mansion be used to make pentacles intended to increase success in hunts for springs and treasures[18], and to work spells for this purpose, and also to injure enemies and protect friends.

Under the name *Al Ghaïr, the Lid,* it is considered unfavorable in every way by the Arabs, especially for familial and other relationships; except for discovery of hostile schemes and for hunts for treasures. Its influence on conjugal happiness is clearly negative in feminine charts. An astrologer can easily verify this with horoscopes in his own collection. Among famous people with the Moon in this Mansion we find Catherine de Medier (especially unhappy in her married life), and Blavatsky (who ran away immediately after her marriage).

Fang, the Chamber frequently symbolized by the silkworm room. The Chinese believe this Mansion encourages achievement of high position or great wealth, especially in old-age, which confers a certain authority to people having the Moon in this Mansion.

Swati, the Sword in the Hindu Zodiac. This *nakshatra* designates a person who gives to others more than he receives, modest but often irascible, fair, sociable, and having a developed business sense.

The Kabbalists who call this Mansion, *Sia, He Who Sustains,* consider it clearly unfavorable, but claim that it protects those who are in misfortune and distress; it "sustains" so to speak in those moments.

MANSION XVI, from 12° 51' 27" to 25° 42' 52" of Libra. — *Alcibene* or *Aiabene* in the Grimoires of Magic which state that the Lunar transit through this Mansion is propitious for charms of enmity. In charts, this position of the Moon signals danger for the reputation and station in life coming from vindictive and jealous persons. The aspects received by the Moon and the whole of the astrological chart always make it possible for this danger to be specified.

Known to the Arabs as *Al Jubana* and *Al Zuban Al-Janubiyyah, the Claws of the Scorpio,* it confers the power of protecting one's self by power of observation and clear judgment. It is considered favorable for stock-breeding, buying and selling of cattle, and speculation, but it is more or less unfavorable for business, marriage, and journeys: impulses in these things are dangerous.

Agrippa, whose interpretations are generally analogous to those of Picatrix and the Arabs, says that this Mansion hinders, i.e., causes delays in marriage and journeys.

Chinese *Hsin, the Heart,* this *siu* is believed to exert a contradictory influence: it gives sociability and amiability but causes disagreements and quarrels in the family.

Hindu *Visakha, the Northern Crown.* This *nakshatra* promotes intelligence and good judgment in the handling of money (which can occasionally take the form of avarice), but inclines to thoughtless commitments. It is the Mansion of pleasant appearance.

Kabbalist *Aiah, Rescue,* it is not believed to promise a happy life, but it is always possible for people born under its influence to evade the blows of fate. So it would seem that this Mansion increases free-will.

We should mention that it is the position of the Moon of Georges Bidault[19].

MANSION XVII, from 25° 42' 53" Libra to 8° 34' 18" Scorpio. — called *Archil* by Picatrix, who judges it favorable for preparing pentacles to make people who have been deceived happy again, to obtain luck, to make buildings lasting, and for travel as well as for charms for friendship.

Arab *Iktil Al Jabbah, the Dome of the Head,* this Mansion is considered favorable for marriage. It enables the native to achieve a responsible position.

Wei, the Dragon's Tail in the system of the Far-East. This *siu* warns the native to be on guard throughout life, since slander is always threatened. Very often this *siu* warns that a greater part of the native's actions will be severely criticized by certain persons in his circle. The chart of Auguste Bebel, leader of the German socialist party, whose Moon is at 4° 44' Scorpio and who frequently suffered condemnation, seems to confirm this attribution; also the nativity of President Truman whose politics aroused violent reactions.

Known in India as *Anuradha,* this Mansion is considered the sign of numerous opportunities in life. It encourages travel and a life far from the place of birth, and warns that the native will rarely be satisfied with his place of residence. It also indicates vanity.

Called *Piah, the Eulogies* by the Hebrews, this Mansion is looked upon favorably. They interpret it as a sign of success in occupations and acquisition of a good position.

MANSION XVIII, from 8° 34' 19" to 21° 25' 44" Scorpio. — In Picatrix it is called *Alchalb* or *Arcalo* which is just a distortion of the Arabic *Al Calb.* "La Clef des Clavicules" recommends using the lunar transit through this Mansion for making pentacles intended to aid conspiracies and for protection from enemies, as well as to work spells to sow discord.

Agrippa says that this Mansion which he calls *Alchas* or *Althob,* causes discord, sedition and conspiracy against princes and potentates; and it is interesting to note that at the moment of the rebellion of February 6, 1934 the Moon was in this Mansion.

The Arabs believe this Mansion, which they call the *Heart of the Constellation Scorpio,* exerts an especially favorable influence for exposing enemies and in times of war; and unfavorable from all other aspects, especially for the family; it is a sign threatening premature death for the mother (often in labor).

Chi, the Basket of the Chinese astrologers, is one of the worst *siu,* since enterprises undertaken by the native never give him the rewards they should. Its symbolism can be compared to *the Tower Struck by Lightning* of the Tarot, since it creates the danger of reversal of situation, most often in shameful circumstances (for example: trial, bankruptcy or scandal). The charts I possess seem to confirm this attribution, since we find the Moon in this Mansion in the horoscope of Marie Antoinette and Alphonse XIII, as well as Kreuger, and even F. de Lesseps whose last days were darkened by the scandal of Panama.

Known in the Hindu Lunar Zodiac as *Jyeshta, the Eldest.* This Mansion indicates an overly self-satisfied man without the talent for making friends. In feminine charts this *nakshatra* seems to incline toward marriage with an older man.

In the Kabbalist system, this Mansion called *Tsiah, Justice* symbolizes above all the idea of reward and punishment — which must be applied specifically to each chart.

We should observe that very often the character of the Mansion seems to be expressed in terms which approximate reality, which are imprecise (a result of the difficulties of translating the cosmic *forces* represented by the Mansions into words). Thus, I have observed that the Moon in this Mansion seems to provoke unfair trials, which corroborates the sense of *judgment* of the Kabbalists, of *discord* and *sedition* in Agrippa and of *conspiracy* in Picatrix.

MANSION XIX, from 21° 25' 45" Scorpio to 4° 17' 10" Sagittarius. — Called *Azarala* and *Exaula* in the Middle Ages. Picatrix advises using the transit of the Moon through this Mansion to make pentacles for armies, for luck in general, and for charms intended to destroy vessels, to help captives escape, and to damage the property of others.

In an article Robert Ambelain adds that fluids must be guarded against and that it is preferable to undertake nothing at this time, since "experience shows the disastrous effect of the Moon in this section of the zodiac."

In the charts of very prominent persons, especially in political charts, it does not indicate a tranquil career; it seems, in this aspect, to share, or reflect, the nature of the preceding Mansion. Among persons with the Moon in this Mansion, we recall Jean Juares, assassinated; William II, who abdicated; A. Tardieu who renounced his seat in parliament; and Marthe Hanau, who died in prison.

Known to the Arabs as *Al Shaulah, the Scorpion's Sting,* this *manazil* is considered favorable for hunting and personal ideas, but unfavorable for commerce and fixity of residence.

Chinese *Tou, the Ladle,* this Mansion favors those who work for others rather than employers and self-employed persons; it is also a good omen for earnings towards the end of life.

In the Hindu system it is *Mula the Root,* sign of a proud man, moderately happy and in fear of the future, but attached to his comfort and ease.

It is also *Quiah, Severity* of the Hebrews, who interpret this Mansion as unfavorable for friendships and children and provoking separation of the native from his children or from his parents.

MANSION XX, from 4° 17' 11" to 17° 8' 36" Sagittarius. — In Medieval Europe it had the name of *Nahaïm.* It promotes eloquence and writings, and the charts of Balzac (whose Moon is at 14° 47' Sagittarius), Gabriele D. Annunzio (Moon in Sagittarius 16°), Francois de Curel (12°) for the writers, and of Ramsay Macdonald (6° 23') and Van Zeeland (16° 52') for politicians confirm the characteristics of this Mansion.

Picatrix advises using the Lunar transit through this part of the heavens to work charms of enmity and to make pentacles against illnesses.

Agrippa says that this Mansion is good for taming wild animals and for protecting prisons, but that it destroys community wealth. He calls it *Abnahaya* or *the Beam.*

Al-Ras-Al-Thuban, the Dragon's Head of the Arab astrologers. This *manazil* promotes love and success in life as much through individual merit as through a woman or women. The fact that this Mansion encourages love, does not mean a happy marriage in most cases; on the contrary, frequently the woman, while useful for business or from the financial point of view, will seek authority in the household. Persons having the Moon in this *manazil,* are better off with a free liason than in married life. It is also an indication of involuntary changes of residence.

Furthermore, according to the Arabs, the passage of the Moon through this Mansion favors constructions and could be chosen for placing the first stone of a building.

Niu, the Cow of the Chinese astrologers. This *siu* promotes trade, although with some risk of loss, and promises improvement in fortune by inheritance or gift. Very often, it is an indication of weakness of the eyes.

In the Hindu system, it is *Purva ashadha, the Front of the Victor,* which marks in the ancient Indian Zodiac the beginning of the series of the twelve constellations of symbolic animals. It makes the native faithful in love, proud, ambitious, often vain, fond of pageantry, but capable at the same time of maintaining a good degree of simplicity.

The Kabbalists consider this Mansion, called *Aiah, the Leader*, the cause of many changes in life, one of which will be around the age of thirty-five years. It also promises a responsible position and often permits the acquisition of a prominent one.

In short, all the traditions agree on the good influence of the Moon in this part of the heavens, even though it is considered peregrine in Sagittarius.

MANSION XXI, from $17° 8' 37''$ Sagittarius to $0°$ Capricorn. — Called *Albelda* by Picatrix, who recommends the lunar passage through this Mansion for making pentacles intended to protect buildings, crops and wealth, and for working charms to break the bonds of love.

Agrippa translates its name, which he spells *Abeda,* as *the Desert,* and recommends using the Moon in this part of the heavens to begin a divorce.

Known to the Arabs by the name of *Caïdat,* this Mansion makes the native imprudent, susceptible and flighty, but is believed to promote travel and earnings, and to exert an influence that hastens and stimulates healing and recovery after illness.

Mo, the Woman, in the Chinese tradition. It is the symbol of vacillating luck, love of children, and loyalty in business.

Uttara Shadha, the Back of the Victor, in the Hindu zodiac. In India, this Mansion is considered the image of a gracious, elegant, well-mannered man, impulsive but obedient to his superiors. It especially seems to favor military men. Hunting instincts and a certain indication to sexual excess are attributed to this *nakshatra,* as to the preceding one.

For the Hebrews, it is *Schiah, the Deliverer* to which they attribute philanthropy and a favorable influence from a financial point of view.

Among historical charts, that of Franz Liszt is particularly representative of this section of the heavens.

This Mansion ends the third septenary of the Lunar Zodiac.

MANSION XXII, from $0°$ to $12° 51' 26''$ Capricorn. — Called *Caaldalbala* or *Caalbeba* by "la Clef des Clavicules," which recommends it for making pentacles intended to stimulate healing and to to work charms to sow discord and bring friendship.

ONE OF THE DISTORTED REPRESENTATIONS OF
THE LUNAR ZODIAC

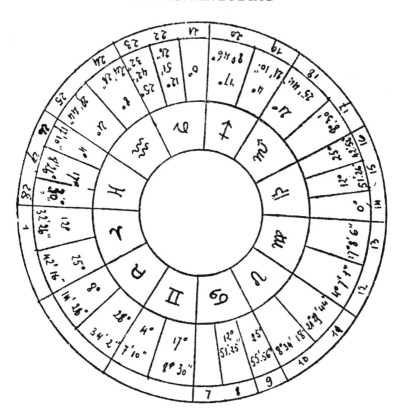

In, spite of the divisions inscribed in the circle, this representation tends to make the boundaries of the Mansions coincide with those of the Solar Signs, which can only be explained by alteration of the traditional data. This distortion existed in every country. In China, for example, an ancient commentator of Ch'u-Li uses, in each Celestial Palace (these will be explained later) the First, Third, and Fifth *siu* as the beginning of the Zodiacal Signs, so that every third Sign contains three *siu* instead of two.

(This plate is taken from Enel's *l'Essai d'Astrologie Kabbalistique*)

Al Sa'ad Al Dhabid, the Fortunate Assassin, among the Arabs. This Mansion is considered one of personal power, which seems to be confirmed by the charts of Hitler, J. Goebbels and many others. According to the Arabs, this *manazil* exerts an unfavorable influence on marriage and on loans of money, but permits a man with the Moon here to escape frequently the consequences of his actions.

Under the name of *Hsü, Emptiness,* this Mansion expresses creative power, a strong will and a sense of justice, in the Middle Empire. It allows advancement in life through the native's own efforts, but exposes him to wounds in wars or riots, and threatens loss of a position attained with difficulty.

Incidentally in remote Chinese antiquity, *siu* XXI and XXII were considered the favorable time for the beginning of marriage; according to Schlegel, this explains why even today Chinese peasants marry only in winter (when the Sun is in that part of the heavens).

I cannot give the Hindu attributions for this Mansion which is called *Abhijit* in India, because between the sixth and eleventh century, the Hindus substituted a series of twenty-seven *nakshatras* for the traditional twenty-eight, while still retaining the latter. Abel Rey[21], believes that the distortions of the Lunar Zodiac made by the Hindus are the crudest of all, and in spite of all my efforts I was not able to obtain the complete Hindu list with the significations for this Mansion.

Among the Hebrews, it is *Thiah, the End of All Things,* an unfavorable Mansion for speculation and trade or for female relations: little luck with women in the family and often the premature death of the mother or the wife.

MANSION XXIII, from $12°51'27''$ to $25°42'52''$ Capricorn. — In Picatrix, it has the name of *Caaldebolach, Caaldebolab* or *Caaldebda.* He recommends it for making pentacles intended to heal illnesses or bind friendship, and for charms to break up love relationships.

Agrippa states that it causes divorce, — which can easily be verified by statistics.

The Arabs who call this Mansion *Al Sad Al Bula, the Fortunate Aviator,* say that it exerts a favorable influence for doctors, soldiers, and politicians, but has an unfavorable effect on everything concerning marriage, children, and contracts. Consequently, no contracts should be signed and no engagements begun when the Moon is in this *manazil.*

The Chinese call this *siu Wei, the Precipice,* and attribute to it an influence in accordance with the symbolism: it is an indication of at least partial loss of wealth towards the end of life. In horary charts, it is a sign of a danger threatening the consultant. It is very probable that this last indication should also be taken into consideration in solar revolutions.

In India, it is *Sravana, the Ear* which promotes fame and popularity, and the love of women. The Hindus consider this Mansion just as favorable for wealth, but this last attribute is very dubious.

For the Kabbalists it is *Casiah,* to which they attributed the power of securing the favor of superiors, but in a more or less intermittent or capricious manner. It is the indication of a career strewn with strife, envy and jealousy; but which could, however, achieve some success through others.

MANSION XXIV, from 25° 42' 53" Capricorn to 8° 34' Aquarius. — In the Middle Ages it was called *Zaaldodothot* and *Caadachot.* Picatrix recommends using the Lunar transit through this Mansion to prepare pentacles intended to promote trade or love, or to triumph over one's enemies; as well as to work charms to damage the actions and possessions of others.

In the Arab Zodiac, it is *Al Sa'd Al Su'd, the Wretched of the Wretched.* It is the sign of an eventful and ultimately rather unhappy career; and the charts of Napoleon I (who had the Moon in Capricorn 29°), of Archduke Rudolf of Hapsburg, hero of Meyrling's drama (whose Moon is in 28° 16' Capricorn), and of many others seem to confirm this attribution. The Arabs consider this *manazil* clearly unfavorable to those responsible for the administration of a country or a city; the higher the position a man occupies in society, the more the unfavorable nature of the Mansion makes itself felt. In horary charts it is nevertheless considered favorable for marriage, plans, enterprises, and friendships.

In China, it is *Che, the Western Wall*[22] which promotes everything having to do with constructions in general and especially the construction of houses. A very great deal of prudence is required in travel by water, which this Mansion disfavors.

In India, this Mansion is called *Dhanishta* or *Shrobistha, Abundance.* It confers a vast knowledge, but also a rather restrained sensitivity; as a result emotional responses generally lack breadth.

The Kabbalists consider this Mansion called *Siah, Strength,* favorable, if the native acts with prudence; but capable of completely overturning his existence, if he tends to act too quickly and carelessly, or in other words, when the *strength* of this Mansion is used without moderation.

MANSION XXV, from 8º 34' 19" to 21º 25' 44" Aquarius.— Called *Caaldabachia* or *Caalda*. In feminine charts it foretells diseases of the uterus. Picatrix recommends using the passage of the Moon through this part of the heavens to prepare pentacles for military success, to hasten vengeance, to protect messengers and aid them to accomplish their duties well, as well as for charms of love and enmity.

"It works as a spell against intercourse," Agrippa states, "and to bind each limb of the man; as a result he is unable to perform the act . . . "

The Arabs call it *Al Sa'd Al Ahbiyah, the Star of the Dungeons.* According to them, it foretells of feminine interventions, which are not always advantaeous, in the native's business affairs; it exerts a very evil influence on pregnancy. Consequently it is not considered favorable except for revenge, and for the effects of medicine.

Py or *Tung Pi (Eastern Wall)* in China. This Mansion has the same nature as the preceding *siu*, but we can add to the indications offered above that *Py* is a sign of inheritance.

Known in India as *Satabhishak, the Great Doctor.* This Mansion is believed to make persons born under its influence courageous, stubborn, capable of triumph over their enemies, but unlucky in business during certain parts of their life, sometimes because of their ambitions or rough manners. They say that illnesses which arise in this lunar division are incurable, and that even Danoantari, the doctor of the gods himself, could not heal the sick during this malefic Mansion.

In the Kabbalist system, it is *Niah, the Light.* It is considered unfavorable for criminals, and for people of loose morals; and favorable to discoveries as well as for the study of sciences; to persons born under its influence, it communicates a lively curiosity for the sciences.

MANSION XXVI, from 21º 25' 45" Aquarius to 4º 17' 10" Pisces.—It is names *Algafarmuth, Algafalbuchor, Algazaldi,* and *Alm.* Picatrix recommends the Lunar transit through this Mansion for making the pentacles of love and of protection against dangers.

Under the name *Al Fargh Al Mukdin, The Upper Hole of the Flask,* the Arabs consider this Mansion favorable for marriage, agriculture, and buying and selling; but unfavorable for ocean voyages.

The Chinese call it *Kei, the Stride* and the determining star for this *siu* in the time of Se-Ma-Ts'ien (104 B.C.) was considered the zero point and the beginning of the series of constellations, exactly as *Revati* is in India. From an astrological viewpoint it signifies the possibility of obtaining a position by the mediation of friends or relations, many deceptions and painful efforts, and finally success.

In India, this Mansion is called *Purva Bhadrapada, the Front of the Blissful.* It is considered a sign of a melancholy, frequently lugubrious imagination, patience, and dignity. From a career point of view this *nakshatra* favors wealth to a certain extent, but this does not mean happiness. On the whole the life is rather sad or difficult. In the list of *nakshatras* given by F. Rolt-Wheeler[24], obedience to women is attributed to this Mansion, as well as a restraint of tender impulses caused by avarice.

Among the Kabbalists, this Mansion has the name *Phias, Eloquence* and is considered favorable for politicians[25], business and works of charity.

MANSION XXVII, from 4° 17' 11" to 17° 8' 36" Pisces. — In the Middle Ages it was known by names similar to those of the preceding Mansion, such as: *Algarfermuth, Algafalbuhor, and Algarfelmucar.* The passage of the Moon through this Mansion seems to facilitate everything having to do with psychism, clairvoyance and spiritism; but we advise against beginning a project when the Moon occupies this part of the heavens, since the matter will be tied up with difficulties, complications and delays.

Picatrix recommends using this transit of the Moon for the preparation of pentacles to Promote trade, friendship, crops, and for fighting illness; as well as for charms "for friendship and enmity, against prisoners and journeys by water."

Among the Arabs this Mansion was known as *Al Fargh Al Thani, the Lower Hole of the Flask.* It imparts love of the outdoors and bad luck with money or incompetence in mangaing it. It is generally believed to exert a favorable influence on harvests, earnings, and marriage, but an unfavorable one on travel, real estate, and loans of money.

The Chinese astrologers' *Lu (Lasso)* is an indication of idealism and of aspirations whose practical applications generally achieve little success, or do not give the expected results. Very often these people demand immediate realization of their visions, which cannot succeed in the form in which they are conceived; or else they expend their energy more in planning than in execution. Among the persons with the Moon in this *siu* we may mention Aristide Briand, who was often accused of pursuing a utopia; Gaston Doumergue whose interim government did not achieve its aim; Marcel Cachin one of the leaders of the communist party; Czar Alexander II of Russia who abolished serfdom, but whose reform did not bring immediate liberty; Chancellor Dollfus; G. Arundade; and Prince F. Youssoupoff, one of the assassins of Rasputin, whose removal did not save the dynasty as the conspirators hoped.

The Chinese, however, believe that the twenty-sixth and twenty-seventh *siu* aid in the maintenance of canals and of wheat granaries; in hunts, border wars, executions and the care of white clothing.

In India, this Mansion is *Uttara Bhadrapada, the Back of the Blissful,* the sign of a retired life, of much uncertainty in the first part of life, and happiness coming from children. From a psychological point of view, it indicates ease with people, a charitable and sensitive nature, and it favors meditations.

Among the Hebrews, this Mansion is *Taddiah, Merit,* to which they attribute a favorable influence for those who act wisely and an unfavorable one for expatriates and usurers.

MANSION XXVIII, from 17º 8' 37" Pisces to 0º Aries. — This last Mansion of the Lunar Zodiac has the name of *Anaxhe.* Picatrix recommends it for the preparation of pentacles for trade, trials, crops and conjugal affection; as well as for charms intended to damage the possessions of others and for sea voyages.

Al Batn Al Hut, The Belly of the Fish, for the Arabs, this *manazil* is considered favorable for conjugal happiness and for business, but unfavorable for sick people. Very often it is a sign of poverty, but also of help in the moment of danger.

Agrippa states that this part of the heavens makes travelers safe during dangerous crossings but causes loss of valuables.

The Chinese *Wei, the Belly.* In the Far East, this Mansion is considered the sign of frequent journeys in the course of life. In feminine charts the presence of the Moon in this Mansion is clearly unfavorable, and the charts I possess seem to prove that this Mansion has some connection with seduction and the birth of a child outside of marriage, or at least with divorce.

In India, it is *Revati, the Extremely Rich,* the sign of popularity, of many virtues, and of courage.

Lastly, the Kabbalists called this Mansion *Oiah, the Sphere,* and they believed it exerted a double influence: externally it indicated a life of struggle, and internally, tranquility and a gentle nature.

Obviously all these significations must be verified, corrected and completed by observation; but my own verifications permit me to say that they are true for the most part.

Agrippa states, "In these twenty-eight Mansions are concealed many secrets of the wisdom of the Ancients, through which they worked many marvels on all those things that are under the influence of the Moon. They assigned to each Mansion the appearances, the images, the characteristics, and the intelligences that ruled it, and performed their operations by their various types of power . . .26."

This account does not pretend to be complete, since the documents dealing with the lunar system are too scattered for one writer to assemble them all. I hope that future research will complete these interpretations. For example, the Lunar Zodiac still exists in Iran and among the Parsis (the second chapter of *Bundeshesah* in the *Zend-Avesta* gives the name of the twenty-eight divisions) and everything would lead us to believe that their interpretations differ from those we have reproduced here.

It can be assumed that the Mansions have an effect not only on the Moon but on all the planets. Brandler-Pracht, who plays the same part in German astrological literature as Julevno does in French[27], calls the degrees: $0°$, $13°$, and $26°$ of cardinal signs $9°$ and $21°$ of fixed signs, and $4°$ and $17°$ of mutable signs, "critical degrees"; he claims that planets in or near those degrees (within about $3°$) exert a stronger influence than if they had no contact with these degrees. Now Brandler-Pracht's "critical degrees" are none other thhan the "cusps" of the Lunar Mansions.

We should add that the Hindus separate these Mansions into masculine and feminine (or positive and negative) exactly as the Zodiacal signs and degrees are separated. Mansions II, III,V,X,XI, XII, XIII, XV, XVIII, XX, XXI, XXII, XXIII, XXVIII are considered masculine, the others feminine. The practical use of these divisions, however, like the planetary rulerships of the Mansions, seems to have been abandoned today by Hindu astrologers, except for determination of the sex of an infant not yet born.

NOTES

[1]"Réflexions sur le Symbolisme des Nombres" in *Astrosophie,* of February 1935, p. 67.

[2]"Des nombres" (vol. II in the collection "Les Maitres de l'Occultisme," Nice, 1946, p.68).

[3]The common feature shared by the Lunar systems in different traditions is the existence of reference stars which mark the boundaries of the twenty-eight divisions. In India, these stars are

called *yogatara*. The names of several Mansions are derived from the names of the stars. The fact that most of these stars are displaced because of the precession of the equinoxes and no longer occupy the Mansions bearing their name, in no way changes the interpretations of these Mansions, since these Mansions, like the Solar Zodiac, are formed by the influence of the Moon spread out over the cross made by the solstices and the equinoxes. We see the same phenomenon here as that of the identity of the names of the constellations and the names of the zodiacal signs which no longer correspond to them.

[4]See the explanation of the Hindu names of the *nakshatras* in our essay "Quelques adaptations locales de l'Astrologie Lunaire" in "Les Cahiers Astrologiques," 1946, #2.

[5]Statistics could prove these attributions. As far as radiesthesia is concerned, for example, the Moon is not in this Mansion in the chart of any radiesthesiologist which I possess, but the cusp of the Fourth Solar House, which governs things hidden in the ground, is here in the chart of M. Brouard as is Jupiter, ruler of his Ascendant; with Emile Christophe this Mansion is in the IV House and contains Mercury, ruler of publications; the Ascendant of M. Lacroix a l'Henri is in this Mansion; it is in the particularly occult Eighth House in the chart of Vicomte Henri de France and contains Neptune, planet of intuition, etc. Since the publication of this book, several radiesthesiologists have written to me saying that they have the Moon in this Mansion.

[6]*La Philosophie Occulte*, Book II, La Haye, 1727, p. 349.

[7]H.P. Blavatsky, *The Secret Doctrine*, vol. IV of the French edition, p. 129.

[8]In any case, all the medieval names of the Mansions come down from the Arabs—the real originators of Astrology in the West.

[9]Born October 15, 1878, a P.M. in Barcelonette.

[10]Note that in India, it is not the seventh, but the Fifth Mansion, since the Hindu Zodiac begins at 26° Aries with *Krittikas*. Even in our day, the *nakshatras* coincide with the position of the stars whose name they bear.

[11]See *l'Astrosophie*, July issue, 1935, p.9.

[12]This chart was published by Ernest Hentges in *Le Grand Nostradamus*, #13, p.33.

[13]Born at Koslan, May 28, 1884, 5:00 A.M.

[14]See *Les Cahiers Astrologiques*, 1946, #3, p. 132.

[15]This chart was cast for the moment of the taking of the Winter Palace, November 7, 1917, 10:40 P.M. in St. Petersburg. The elements of the chart, which have never been published are:

MC — 28° 30' Aries	Venus — 0° 44' Capricorn
XI — 12° 24' Gemini	Mars — 2° 56' Virgo
XII — 22° 33' Cancer	Jupiter — 9° 12' Gemini
ASC — 20° 34' Leo	Saturn — 14° 14' Leo
II — 5° 45' Virgo	Uranus — 19° 49' Aquarius
III — 27° 1' Virgo	Neptune — 7° 7' Leo
Sun — 14° 52' 32" Scorpio	Pluto — 5° 4' Cancer
Moon — 27° 6' Leo	Part of Fortune — 2° 48' Gemini
Mercury — 17° 22' Scorpio	North Node — 3° 55' Capricorn

[16]Certainly all the names of the Mansions played a part in medieval magic; in any case they belong more to magic than Astrology. But I hope that in the future, when study of the influence of the Mansions will be more widespread, one of these names will be finally chosen to designate each Mansion, as Aries designates the first sign of the Solar Zodiac, Taurus the second, etc.

[17]This chart was published in #17, p.4 of *Le Grand Nostradamus*.

[18]In other words, this Mansion should have something in common with the Second, as regards radiesthesia, although this "hunt for treasures," must be understood in the broadest sense — which explains the presence of the Moon in this part of the heavens in the charts of Le Verrier, Blavatsky and many other seekers of scientific or spiritual treasure.

[19]Born October 5, 1899, 3 P.M. at Moulins.

[20]"Le Calendrier Lunaire mensuel" in *Votre Destin*, April 5 issue, 1935.

[21]*La Science Orientale avant les Grecs*, Paris, 1930, p. 383.

[22]The Chinese represented the constellation Pegasus as a building whose Western Wall was *Che* and whose Eastern Wall was *Py*, the following *siu*. Frequently the two Mansions are counted as

one, which transforms the twenty-eight *siu* into twenty-seven. Earlier we noted the same distortion made by the Hindus.

[23]Agrippa, *La Philosophie Occulte,* Book II, p. 353.

[24]*Cours de'Astrologie,* Lesson 66.

[25]We can cite as example the chart of Victor Emmanuel (whose Moon is in $27°19'$ Aquarius) who emerged relatively unharmed, from the chaotic events Italy passed through during his reign. Napoleon III also had the Moon in this Mansion.

[26]*La Philosophie Occulte,* p. 354.

[27]Vol. I of the 1925 edition, p. 58.

RULERSHIP OF THE MANSIONS
IN HINDU ASTROLOGY

In our Occidental tradition, each quarter of the Lunar Zodiac is governed by the same sequence of the seven planets known to the Ancients; this is to a certain extent analogous to the planetary week. The Hindu astrologers, however, who now work with a distorted Lunar Zodiac of twenty-seven *nakshatras,* have invented three series of nine rulers for them.

It is impossible to adapt this system to our Occidental methods, because it is really not a Zodiacal system (in the usual meaning of that word), but a sidereal one: in actuality, the circle of twenty-seven *nakshatras* follows the movement of the precession of the equinoxes and the figures given below should correct the deviation between our *gamma* point and $0°$ Aries of the Hindu Zodiac[1], ($22°$ 26' 18" for January 1, 1900; and $23°$ 5' 39" for January 1, 1947). Whatever the case may be, these are the rulerships of the *nakshatras:*

The South Node of the Moon or Cauda (which the Hindus call *Kethu* and which they elevate to the level of a planet) governs the First, Tenth, and Nineteenth *nakshatras* (i.e., the space between $0°$ and $13°$ 20' in Aries, Leo, and Sagittarius).

Venus rules the Second, Eleventh, and Twentieth *nakshatras* located from $13°$ 20' to $26°$ 40' Aries, Leo, Sagittarius;

The Sun is the ruler of the three following divisions, i.e., the Third, Twelfth, and Twenty-first;

The Moon assumes rulership of the Fourth, Thirteenth, and Twenty-second *nakshatras* (occupying the space from $10°$ to $23°$ 20' Taurus, Virgo, and Capricorn);

Mars governs the Fifth, Fifteenth, and Twenty-third of these constellations (*constellations* because they are really asterisms designated in the heavens by the fixed stars);

The North Node or Caput (which the Hindus call *Rahu,* and which they treat like a planet) rules the three following divisions, i.e., the Sixth, Fifteenth, and Twenty-fourth (from 6° 40' to 20° Gemini, Libra and Aquarius);

Jupiter follows as ruler of Seventh, Sixteenth and Twenty-fifth *nakshatras* (which occupy the space in the heavens from 3° 20' to 16° 40' Cancer, Scorpio and Pisces);

Lastly, Mercury closes each series of nine *nakshatras.*

Although, to my mind, this is a distorted Lunar Zodiac, these rulerships are by no means abstractions without practical import. On the contrary, Hindu astrologers draw from this system many practical applications some of which appear to be verifiable daily.

Furthermore, a curious method of progression, completely unknown in France, called *Dasas,* derives directly from this system.

This technique is based on the age or the time attributed to each *nakshatra* and to its ruler, attributions which may be summarized in the following table of relationships:

	DASA	Length
I, X, XIX	Kethu (South Node)	Seven years
II, XI, XX	Venus	Twenty years
III, XII, XXI	Sun	Six years
IV, XIII, XXII	Moon	Ten years
V, XIV, XXIII	Mars	Seven years
VI, XV, XXIV	Rahu (North Node)	Eighteen years
VII, XVI, XXV	Jupiter	Sixteen years
VIII, XVII, XXVI	Saturn	Nineteen years
IX, XVIII, XXVII	Mercury	Seventeen years

The position of the Moon at the moment of birth determines which planet rules at that instant, and the planets which follow influence the native at the corresponding ages, according to the table above[2].

Let us use, for example, a birth on July 9, 1900. Our western ephemerides place the Moon at 248° 46', from which the precession must be deducted to locate it in the Hindu Lunar Zodiac, where it falls at about 226° 13' 15", i.e., in the seventh *nakshatra* ruled by Saturn. Since the total area of this *nakshatra,* from 3° 20' to 16° 40' Scorpio, is equivalent to nineteen years, the native will be influenced by that planet for about seven months and twenty-five days only, which corre-

A HINDU ZODIAC

The outer circle is that of the twelve signs; the figures on the inside are those of the Nakshatras.

sponds to the arc separating the Moon from the following division. Thereafter the life will be governed for seventeen years by Mercury Dasa, which at the age of seventeen years, seven months, twenty-five days will give its place to Kethu Dasa, and so forth.

Each of these periods is, in turn, subdivided into nine smaller ones called *Bhukthies,* ruled by one of the nine planets (including Rahu & Kethu, and Hindu astrologers claim that the events which occur always reflect exactly the nature of these two planets (the ruler of the *nakshatra,* and the ruler of the subdivision). They believe, the combination of these two rulers produces an effect similar to our two planet conjunction.

In the *Nakshatras* of Kethu — 7 years:

Kethu rules	0 years	4 months	27 days
Venus rules	1 year	2 months	0 days
Sun rules	0 years	4 months	6 days
Moon rules	0 years	7 months	0 days
Mars rules	0 years	4 months	27 days
Rahu rules	1 year	0 months	18 days
Jupiter rules	0 years	11 months	6 days
Saturn rules	1 year	1 month	9 days
Mercury rules	0 years	11 months	27 days

In the Venus *nakshatras* — 20 years:

Venus rules	3 years	4 months	
Sun rules	1 year	0 months	0 days
Moon rules	1 year	8 months	0 days
Mars rules	1 year	2 months	0 days
Rahu rules	3 years	0 months	0 days
Jupiter rules	2 years	8 months	0 days
Saturn rules	3 years	2 months	0 days
Mercury rules	2 years	10 months	0 days
Kethu rules	1 year	2 months	0 days

In the Sun *nakshatras* — 6 years:

Sun rules	0 years	3 months	18 days
Moon rules	0 years	6 months	0 days
Mars rules	0 years	4 months	6 days
Rahu rules	0 years	10 months	24 days
Jupiter rules	0 years	9 months	18 days
Saturn rules	0 years	11 months	12 days
Mercury rules	0 years	10 months	6 days
Kethu rules	0 years	4 months	6 days
Venus rules	1 year	0 months	0 days

In the Moon *nakshatras* — 10 years:

Moon rules	0 years	10 months	0 days
Mars rules	0 years	7 months	0 days
Rahu rules	1 year	6 months	0 days
Jupiter rules	1 year	4 months	0 days
Saturn rules	1 year	7 months	0 days
Mercury rules	1 year	5 months	0 days

In the Moon *nakshatras* — 10 years:

Kethu rules	0 years	7 months	0 days
Venus rules	1 year	8 months	0 days
Sun rules	0 years	6 months	0 days

In the Mars *nakshatras* — 7 years:

Mars rules	0 years	4 months	27 days
Rahu rules	1 year	0 months	18 days
Jupiter rules	0 years	11 months	6 days
Saturn rules	1 year	1 month	9 days
Mercury rules	0 years	11 months	27 days
Kethu rules	0 years	4 months	27 days
Venus rules	1 year	2 months	0 days
Sun rules	0 years	4 months	6 days
Moon rules	0 years	7 months	0 days

In the Rahu *nakshatras* — 18 years:

Rahu rules	2 years	8 months	12 days
Jupiter rules	2 years	4 months	24 days
Saturn rules	2 years	10 months	6 days
Mercury rules	2 years	6 months	18 days
Kethu rules	1 year	0 months	18 days
Venus rules	3 years	0 months	0 days
Sun rules	0 years	10 months	24 days
Moon rules	1 year	6 months	0 days
Mars rules	1 year	0 months	18 days

In the Jupiter *nakshatras* — 16 years:

Jupiter rules	2 years	1 month	18 days
Saturn rules	2 years	6 months	12 days
Mercury rules	2 years	3 months	6 days
Kethu rules	0 years	11 months	6 days
Venus rules	2 years	8 months	0 days
Sun rules	0 years	9 months	18 days
Moon rules	1 year	4 months	0 days
Mars rules	0 years	11 months	6 days
Rahu rules	2 years	4 months	24 days

In the Saturn *nakshatras* — 19 years:

Saturn governs	3 years	0 months	3 days
Mercury governs	2 years	8 months	9 days

In the Saturn *nakshatras* — 19 years:

Kethu governs	1 year	1 month	9 days
Venus governs	3 years	2 months	0 days
Sun governs	0 years	11 months	12 days
Moon governs	1 year	7 months	0 days
Mars governs	1 year	1 month	9 days
Rahu governs	2 years	10 months	6 days
Jupiter governs	2 years	6 months	12 days

In the Mercury *nakshatras* — 17 years:

Mercury rules	2 years	4 months	27 days
Kethu rules	0 years	11 months	27 days
Venus rules	2 years	10 months	0 days
Sun rules	0 years	10 months	6 days
Moon rules	1 year	5 months	0 days
Mars rules	0 years	11 months	26 days
Rahu rules	2 years	6 months	18 days
Jupiter rules	2 years	3 months	6 days
Saturn rules	2 years	8 months	9 days

Each of these subdivisions may be divided again into *Antaraus* or *Inter-Periods,* which permits the date of each event to be determined more precisely — but these indications are sufficient to demonstrate the use to which the Hindus put the Lunar Zodiac.

There are many other techniques using this rulership of the *nakshatras,* but it is impossible to include them here without giving a more or less complete description of Hindu astrology.*

NOTES

[1]Other figures for the deviation between the starting point of our Tropical Zodiac and that of the Hindu Sidereal Zodiac have been offered by different authors in the West, but the ones I have given here are certainly more accurate. They were given to me, along with other material in this chapter, by M. Gabriel Lescuré, captain of the port of Pondicherry, an experienced astrologer.

[2]The sum of the ages of the nine planets and of a series of nine *nakshatras* is one hundred twenty years, given by the Hindus as the *normal* duration of human life.

---

*See *Hindu Predictive Astrology* by B.V. Raman and *Directional Astrology of the Hindus* by V.G. Rele for further elucidation. ED.

SOME NOTES ON THE CHINESE SYSTEM

We have already mentioned the profound differences which exist between the ancient Chinese system of unequal *siu,* and the equal Mansions whose significations were given in the preceding chapter. The Chinese system merits our attention.

The name *Zodiac* cannot really be applied to it, since the Zodiac is the zone of the ecliptic, while the Chinese based their system on the equator, and not on the ecliptic like our Chaldean-Greek-Arab tradition. So in speaking of the "Lunar Zodiac" in the Far-East, we must never forget that it represents the equatorial band and not the true Zodiac.

The inequality of these *siu* undoubtedly corresponds to variations observed in the planetary influence rather than to astronomical causes. The astrological basis of these divisions leaves every astronomer perplexed.

"It is very surprising," said Ideler[1], "that the intervals of the twenty-eight Chinese divisions show such great inequalities; some of them less than $2°$ 42' in equatorial width, very near to others with more than $30°$, even in ancient times . . . I was never fortunate enough to discover the principle which determined the choice of these stars" (which mark the limits of the *siu*).

Biot thinks that twenty of the *siu* are the equatorial stars corresponding to the great circumpolar ones; and the other eight were the pointer stars to the cardinal positions in the twenty-fourth and twelfth centuries B.C. No argument could be raised against this opinion since it is supported by extensive evidence; but it still does not explain the purpose or the cause for this division. No one would invent a very complicated system solely for the pleasure of transposing circumpolar stars to the equator, if this transposition did not have more profound reasons, such as the variation of planetary influences.

Besides, even where they bear the names of the stars and constellations (as do certain Occidental and Arab Mansions) the *siu* occasionally show very visible deviations of 2°, 3°, 4° and even more from the great circumpolar stars.

Lastly, numerous texts confirm that the reasons for the divisions are based on Astrology. For example the Sixteenth Mansion, *siu* is considered the 'heart' of the Lunar Zodiac, just as the sign Leo is the 'heart' of the Solar Zodiac. It remains to be seen if the affliction of a vital point of the horoscope in this *siu* (4° 50'–9° 30' Libra) always has something to do with cardiac illnesses. In a horoscope in my collection, the native, who suffered from a chronic disease of the heart, had his Ascendant exactly in that part of the heavens. A coincidence?

This system of unequal *siu* also seems to be much less stable. Some documents combine two *siu* (Se-Ma Ts'ien for instance, counts *Tsan* and *Tse* as only one division), so that we get an equatorial "Zodiac" of twenty-seven signs, just as the Arabs, the Berbers, and others have.

On the other hand, the Chinese system can be considered a sidereal Zodiac, depending more on fixed stars than on cardinal points; the displacement of the pole explains the change through the ages in the size of certain *siu* based on latitudinal stars. When, in 1683 by the order of Emperor K'ang-hi, the Jesuits constructed the table of co-ordinates of the determining stars, Pi Gambil says, "They should have put *Tsan* before *Tse*. It was not done, so that the order of the ancient catalogue would be retained."[2]

Judging from the value of the longitudes, the natural order would in fact be: *Pi, Tsan, Tse, Tsing,* etc. Already by 1280, under the Yuën, Koch-king, measuring the length of the *siu Tse* found only 0° 5', because the two stars *Tse (Lambda Orionis)* and *Tsan (delta Orionis)* which mark the boundaries of this Mansion, cross the meridian almost simultaneously. These two stars play a unique role in Chinese Astrology.

This system may be summarized by the following table:

Chinese Name	Constellations	Approx. Length	Remarks
1. Mao	Pleiades	9° 39'	According to Whitney, the *siu Mao* begins with *eta Tauri.* The *Mao-Pi* division was marked by *x-Librae.*
2. Pi — the Snare	Taurus	18° 6'	According to Whitney, this Mansion was connected with *Aldebaran* in all the ancient systems.
3. Tse	Head of Orion	2° 19'	The constellation Orion gives birth to two *siu Tse* and *Tsan.*

Chinese Name	Constellations	Approx. Length	Remarks
4. Tsan — the Warrior	Orion	2° 48'	The reference star for *Tsan* varied in different centuries and was successively, *alpha, gamma, delta, zeta, epsilon, kappa,* and *beta Orionis.* We should note that among the Arabs, this Mansion was always marked by stars in the constellation Gemini.
5. Tsing — the Well	Gemini	26° 28'	The reference stars varied throughout different eras, but always belonged to the constellation Gemini.
6. Kwe — the Ghost	Cancer	8°	According to L. de Saussure, already under the *Han,* astrologers could not differentiate between systems from different eras, which explains all the gaps in this table.
7. Liu — the Willow		22° 40'	Note that *Liu* also has the sense of *halt* or *stop;* and immediately after the summer solstice which this *siu* ends with, the Sun changes direction; the etymology of this division underscores the Sun's halt in its rise in the heavens.
8. Hsing	Hydra	9°	In the primitive system the eighth *siu* began with *alpha Hydra* (Alphard), while the Ninth was designated by the stars *kappa, lambda, mu* and other stars of the same constellation in succession
9. Chang — Bended Bow	Hydra	16° 39'	
10. I or Yi	Crater	15° 20'	According to Whitney, this *siu* began with *alpha, beta, crateris,* etc. in succession.
11. Chin — Servitude		14° 13'	Whitney thinks that the constellation Corvus is at the beginning of this Mansion.
12. Chio — the Two Horns	Virgo	11° 18'	These *siu* were respectively marked by *Arcturus* (Ta Chio) and *Spica* (Kang). We should mention that *Chio* is often called *Primum ver,* since the star with that name served as a reference for *Li-Ch'ouen* (expression designating a Celestial demi-palace) before the equinox.
13. Kang — of the Dragon Ch'en	Boötes	9°	
14. Ti — the Root		14° 30'	Whitney thinks that, in all traditions, this Mansion rose from the Pincers of Scorpio.
15. Fang — the Chamber		4° 50'	According to Schlegel, the equidistance between *Ti* and *Fang* was marked by A. 766 *Tauri.*
16. Hsin — the Heart	Heart of Scorpio	4° 40'	*Fang* and *Hsin* were often combined under the name of *Ha.*
17. Wei — Tail of the Dragon	Scorpio	17° 49'	This system shows an assymmetry between opposing *siu.* According to Biot, the assymmetry between the second and seventeenth amounts to 9'; between the third and eighteenth, 26'; between the sixth and the twentieth, 47'; between the tenth and the twenty-fourth, 16' and between the eleventh and the twenty-fifth Mansion, 1° 1'.

Chinese Name	Constellations	Approx. Length	Remarks
18. Chi — the Basket		6° 43'	Whitney attributes the origin of this Mansion to the constellation Sagittarius.
19. Tou — the Ladle	Sagittarius	30° 34'	
20. Niu — the Cow		6° 50'	Whitney assumes that this Mansion derives from the constellation Capricorn, although the Hindus associated their corresponding Mansion with the constellation *Lyra*.
21. Niu or Mo — the Woman	Aquila	9° 40'	
22. Hsu — Emptiness	Aquila	8° 54'	
23. Loei — the Precipice	Aquarius	18° 48'	According to Whitney, this *siu* was marked in different eras successively by *alpha aquarii* and by *theta* and *epsilon* Pegasi.
24. Che — the Building rather, the Western Wall of the building	Pegasus	16° 4'	
25. Py or Tung-Pi	Pegasus	12° 10'	According to L. de Saussure, the size of *Py* is 18° 6'. We notice that *Che* and *Py*, in China as in India, are two halves of Pegasus. Chinese Astrology represents this floor by a ritual building.
26. Kei — the Stride	Andromeda	18° 30'	According to Whitney, the boundary of this Mansion was marked primitively by *zeta Andromedae*.
27. Lu	Aries	9° 8'	E. Chavaunes translates *Lu* as "Harvest Basket." The ideograph of this *siu* is a woman bearing a basket of grass on her head.
52. Wei — the Belly		15° 20'	

This table, which is far from complete and probably contains some error since every sinologist gives a different version, can give an idea of the profoundly original Chinese system. On the other hand, in spite of the well-known traditionalism and conservatism of the Chinese, this system has undergone many transformations. In the course of the centuries we find a whole series of reforms which generally coincide with changes in dynasty, but which manage to completely subvert the established conceptions and doctrines. And since all life in China was "ruled" by the heavens, these reforms had their repercussions on rites and customs. We know, for example, that the place of honor in different epochs was sometimes on the left, sometimes on the right. So everything would lead us to believe that this is just a consequence of the fluctuations in the doctrine of the Lunar Zodiac which accepted *Mao* sometimes, and *Lu Wei* other times as the equinoctial *siu*.

All the *siu* are divided into four groups:

The *Eastern Palace* which begins with Kio, includes *siu* 12, 13, 14, 15, 16, 17, and 18 and extends over 70° 50';

The *Northern Palace,* composed of *siu* 19, 20, 21, 22, 23, 24, 25 and extending over 101° 10';

The *Western Palace,* composed of *siu* 26, 27, 28, 1, 2, 3, and 4 covering 75° 40';

The *Southern Palace,* which covers the *siu* 5, 6, 7, 8, 9, 10, 11, or 112° 20'.

As may be seen, the Palaces bear the name of the opposite cardinal points. For us in the West the characteristic feature of spring is the position of the Sun at the vernal point, but for the Chinese the season is most clearly announced by the full Moon in the autumn equinox. This point of view may explain the importance of Lunar Astrology in general, and of Lunar eclipses in particular in the Celestial Empire.

Although the following belongs to the field of astronomy and not astrology, we should mention that the small *palaces* (spring and autumn) are in a proportion to the large *palaces* of 73 to 107 along the equator or 75 to 105 along the ecliptic, i.e., they reproduce exactly the ratio of longest day of the solstice to shortest night, as L. de Saussure has observed[3].

Each of the cardinal palaces is symbolized by an animal and a color.

For spring, the Green Dragon;

For summer, the Red Bird;

For autumn, the White Tiger;

For winter, the Black Tortoise or the Dark Warrior.

Uranographically, the Dragon and the Tiger are merely Scorpio and Orion; the Bird and the Tortoise have no sidereal correspondences and both are thought to fill a large *palace*. No color or symbolic animal is attached to the central palace — polar region and symbol of the absolute, the metaphysical and initiatory center — because it represents the unformed world.

The concept of the five celestial palaces, which is represented on the earth by the Middle Empire surrounded by the four cardinal points, is the keystone of the Chinese Cosmology and Astrology. This idea may be expressed by the principle that each state is a complete image of the heavens, and although it is governed by some dominating planet and affinitive sign or other, in its parts a complete Zodiac can be found. France, for example, is undeniably under the dominant influence of the Signs Leo and Aries, but Paris is related to the sign Virgo, the Cote d'Azur to Gemini, etc. *Le Zodiaque de Paris* published in 1912 by V. Piobb in the *"Annees psychiques et occultistes,"* gives a clear idea of this conception. This Zodiac represents the correspondences of different regions of Paris to different signs, showing that the peculiarities of one *arondissement* or another are in accord with the nature of the sign that corresponds to it.

Chinese Astrology, seeking to penetrate directly to the essence of things, deeply homogeneous and symbolic, considers the Universe, the State, and the Human Being as organic unities. The same key opens up the mystery of nature, determines the action of the emperor, and permits penetration of the human soul. This homogeneous conception obliges us to avoid becoming too involved with the system of unequal *siu,* because it would force us to explore the question of the palaces and even of the symbolism of fixed stars, of the dodecatomories and the zodiacal signs, — Chinese Astrology could be compared to a structure whose parts all touch and complete each other.

An example may give an idea of the interdependence of the different parts. The sign Aries bears the name *Cock* because this bird with its crow announces the sunrise and the birth of the day — which represents the vernal phase in the diurnal cycle. The character it imparts to those born under its influence is that of the Fighter. *Mao* is represented symbolically by *an open door* (at the springtime of life), while the autumnal equinox is *a closed door.* By analogy, the person designated by *Mao* cannot keep a secret, he can exteriorize easily and is characterized by all the analogies with an open door which lets the interior be seen. Contrarily, *the closed door* of the autumnal equinox makes the native reserved, able to hide his thoughts and conceal what goes on inside him.

To conclude these notes on the ancient Chinese system, we should add that it must have had a great importance in Astrology, but it is even more difficult to adapt to our Western astrological methods than the Hindu system, since our Astrology is zodiacal while the Chinese system is exclusively equatorial.

Although a practical application of it would meet with obstacles, and in any case we can by no means recommend it, nevertheless we felt it was necessary to describe this system in order to give an idea of all the problems of Lunar Astrology.

NOTES

[1]Cited by L. de Saussure: "Les Origines de l'Astronomie Chinoise," p.47.
[2]Cited by L. de Saussure: "Les Origines de l'Astronomie Chinoise," p.143.
[3]"Les Origines de l'Astronomie Chinoise," p. 101.

THE TWENTY-EIGHT LUNAR HOUSES

Whereas the twenty-eight Mansions are fixed and always start from $0°$ Aries; the Lunar Houses are only the phases of the Moon, and are calculated from the precise point of the conjunction of the Luminaries. Modern astrologers ignore this point, but it was very important for all the astrologers of the Middle Ages, who almost always noted it on charts and took it into consideration in studying progression. This point was even occasionally considered the *hyleg,* i.e., the vital point in the life. Its importance is confirmed by all of tradition.

"In a revolution or year chart," says Claudius Ptolemy in the fifty-eighth aphorism of this "Centiloquy," "note how far from the Ascendant is the place in the Zodiac where the last conjunction of the Sun and Moon occurred, since when the Ascendant arrives at this place by progression, some event will happen . . . "

In short, the point of the conjunction of the Luminaries, which is the point of departure for the Lunar Houses, just as the Ascendant is for the Solar Houses, is so important that some astrologers even today rectify natal charts on the basis of the new Moon before birth.

The system of Lunar Houses is a means of evaluating the variations of influences of the Luminaries in proportion to the distance separating them.

There is substantial proof of variations in lunar influence according to phase, which is not disputed. The relationships between the phases of our satellite and plant growth are too well known to need mention, but science has recorded indisputable evidence of the variation of the lunar influence on humans. It has been observed, for example, in the incubation of intermittent fevers in India, the Balearic Islands, South America, etc. Dr. Emile Legrain[1] has disclosed that new outbreaks of these fevers begin eight out of ten times in the few days preceding or following the new Moon (conjunction of the luminaries) and very rarely at the full Moon. Bilious fevers are aggravated at the same time; ulcers in the last quarter of the new Moon; varicose veins at the new Moon, as well as shingles. Epileptic fits are more common at Full Moon. In 1935, in the magazine "Demain,"[2] G.L'Brahy published a very well documented article on multiple manifestations of lunar influence, and we feel it is unnecessary to overload this text with examples of the influence of phases, which the reader can find in that article or in many others.

Observations demonstrate overwhelmingly the nature of the Moon as it is described by tradition. For example: our satellite has always been represented as a moist and cold principle; Dr. G.E. Maag[3] researching two lunar periods from 1881 to 1899, and from 1899 to 1918, showed that the influence of the Moon lowered temperature.

"The cold effect associated with the Moon as well as the effect of lowering of barometric pressure are both more intense during the Full Moon phase; the cold effect is otherwise more observable when the culmination point of the Moon is low and when it is at apogee (with diminution of the effect of lowering of barometric pressure at the same time); and lastly, the effect of lowering barometric pressure is stronger when the culmination point of the Moon is higher and when it is at perigee (with diminution of the cold effect at the same time)."

If most of the statements of the Ancients on the subject of the Moon have proved verifiable through scientific research, there is no reason for neglecting the whole system of Mansions and Houses.

Like the Mansions, the Lunar Houses numbered twenty-eight, twenty-nine, thirty, and even thirty-one among different peoples in different eras. Very often they were called "days," "courts," and even "mansions," but we prefer the term "Lunar Houses," because here we we are dealing with a system that corresponds very much to the universally accepted Solar Houses.

Following the Arabs' example, the Middle Ages measured the Houses in an approximate manner by days; but if a system of equal Houses is used, a Lunar House must equal one day one hour 18.7 minutes (which is 1/28th of the synodic Lunar revolution) and not twenty-four hours.

But in antiquity there were Lunar Houses that followed the phases of the Moon. The more the Moon was visible, the greater the size of the House. The Chaldeans, who invented arithmetic and geometric progressions, left documents dealing with this increase in Houses in proportion to the age of the Moon. For the most part, most traditional scholars see in this first attempts at approximative evaluations of Lunar movement. But, knowing the degree of development of the astronomical observations of the Chaldeans, it is impossible to see anything in this progression but Lunar Houses, and not ephemerides as certain Assyriologists would have it.

"This table of Lunar Light, which, do not forget, forms part of the tablets of the library of Assurbanipal, at Nineveh (mid-seventh century), but which could of course be a copy or even an older original, is highly suggestive," says Abel Rey[4]. It is very difficult, perhaps impossible, that without astronomically precise instruments they were able to hit upon these arithmetical proportions of light increase/decrease by observation alone. It is a safe guess that this is a reduction to logical order of the more or less approximate empiric data. Onto the rude measures it has at hand, the mind projects the concept of a regular law of increase, of a rhythmic progression of lighting of the Moon . . ."

". . .Its own movement is from about $8°$ 30' to $15°$ 30' during the fifteen days of increase and inversely from $15°$ 30' to $8°$ 30' during decrease; this makes an average difference of $7°$ in fourteen days, or 30' per day. This number is adopted as the basis of the arithmetic progression of the Moon, positive or negative. Thus it would cover $8°$ 30' on the first day of the new Moon, $8°$ 30' plus 30' on the second, etc. . . . "

It is unnecessary to formulate all the criticisms against the tendencies to interpret documents dealing with this progression, as first attempts at construction of ephemerides: a people who succeeded in dividing the Lunar disc in two hundred forty parts would observe that the Moon never advances with the speed of $8°$ a day. This progression is that of the twenty-eight Houses which could be represented by the following table:

HOUSE	SIZE	FROM	TO	
I	$8°$ 30'	$0°$	$8°$ 30'	after conjunction of the luminaries
II	$9°$	$8°$ 30'	$17°$ 30'	—
III	$9°$ 30'	$17°$ 30'	$27°$	—
IV	$10°$	$27°$	$37°$	—
V	$10°$ 30'	$37°$	$47°$ 30'	—
VI	$11°$	$47°$ 30'	$58°$ 30'	—
VII	$11°$ 30'	$58°$ 30'	$70°$	—
VIII	$12°$	$70°$	$82°$	—
IX	$12°$ 30'	82	$94°$ 30'	—
X	$13°$	$94°$ 30'	$107°$ 30'	—
XI	$13°$ 30'	$107°$ 30'	$121°$	—

XII	14°	121°	135°	—
XIII	14° 30'	135°	149° 30'	—
XIV	44° 30' (approx.)	149° 30' after conjunction of luminaries	until the moment of their opposition	
XV	44° 30' (approx.)	point of opposition of luminaries	to 149° 30' from the next conjunction of luminaries	
XVI	14° 30'	149° 30'	135°	before next conjunction of luminaries
XVII	14°	135°	121°	—
XVIII	13° 30'	121°	107° 30'	—
XIX	13°	107° 30'	94° 30'	—
XX	12° 30'	94° 30'	82°	—
XXI	12°	82°	70°	—
XXII	11° 30'	70°	58° 30'	—
XXIII	11°	58° 30'	47° 30'	—
XXIV	10° 30'	47° 30'	37°	—
XXV	10°	37°	27	—
XXVI	9° 30'	27°	17° 30'	—
XXVII	9°	17° 30'	8° 30'	—
XXVIII	8° 30'	8° 30'	conjunction of the luminaries	—

We believe this system of Lunar Houses is more in line with reality, since the malefic nature of the First and Twenty-eighth Houses which we will demonstrate in the next chapter does not seem to be felt beyond 8° 30' from the point of exact conjunction.

In this system, the tenth House corresponds to the First quarter, with the Moon increasing through the first fourteen Houses and decreasing through the last fourteen, while the third quarter corresponds to the Nineteenth House.

Later we will describe the simple method for determining, in each individual case, the Lunar House in which the night Luminary is found; for the present, note that if the Moon is increasing, we must work from the conjunction of the Luminaries preceding birth; if, on the other hand, the Moon has passed the opposition to the Sun and is decreasing, we must work from the conjunction following the moment of birth.

Documents on the variation of lunar influence are rarer and more fragmented than those corresponding to the Mansions. These documents may be summarized in the following manner:

The first quarter of the Moon is moist and confers a sanguine temperament;

The second is hot and gives a nervous temperament;
The third is dry and governs the bilious temperament;
The fourth is cold and symbolizes the lymphatic temperament[5].

"When the Moon is in its first quarter, i.e., beginning to separate from the Sun with which it was in conjunction," Ptolemy says[6], "the humors swell the body, until the end of the second quarter; but when the Moon moves into the two other quarters, the humors diminish and decrease . . ."

"The Moon is a significator of different materials," he adds in aphorism sixty-one of the *Centiloquy,* "which compose the body in such a manner that they actually undergo the movement of the Moon on the increase or decrease . . ."

The Moon on the increase exerts a good influence for all sorts of open activities pursued in the light of day. The experiments made by Henri Copin[7] prove that broods and plantings generally give more abundant hatches and crops when they are made when the Moon is increasing, especially in the first quarter. In birth charts, it is considered more favorable than the waning Moon, which increases the force of malefics according to astrologers of the Middle Ages; this second half of the Lunar month favors more hidden activities.

This tradition undoubtedly traces back to far antiquity, because the Phoenicians divided the Lunar month in two parts: fourteen days of the White Moon (increase) and fourteen days of the Black Moon (decrease).

Lastly, according to Hebraic tradition, the first and third Lunar week should be consecrated to acts of charity, and the second and the fourth to acts of justice.

Ancient astrologers took the phases of the Moon into consideration when interpreting charts — even those who did not leave a line devoted to Lunar Astrology. Regiomontanus, for example, a "classical" astrologer of the Fifteenth Century, made a big distinction between the effects formed by the Moon increasing and those of the Moon decreasing. Here are some of his observations:

"The Moon increasing in aspect to Mercury after an aspect with Jupiter foretells that the child will be an orphan, and will marry a rich widow . . ."[8]

"The decreasing Moon in aspect to Mercury after an aspect with Saturn causes stuttering and sometimes deafness; it is a sign of weakness in the organism and a high sensitivity to chills . . ."

"The increasing Moon in aspect to Saturn foretells much unhappiness in the life: the mother of the native is threatened with early widowhood . . ."

"The decreasing Moon in aspect with Mercury after an aspect with Venus signifies loss of situation and of health as the natural effects of unleashed passions . . ."

Quotations and evidence on the variation of the lunar influence according to its phases could be multiplied indefinitely. Tradition throughout the world is unanimous in proclaiming it. Ancient doctors paid attention to it and left abundant observations. For example, a tumor must not be operated on when the Moon is in the first quarter or it could lead to recurrence with complications. Unless absolutely urgent, an operation should not be done when the luminaries are in square, or in other words, with the Moon in IX, X, XIX and XX Lunar Houses.

"Take advantage of the Moon to cure the eyes, when it is augmented in light (increasing) and free of the aspect of malignant (malefic) planets, — #39 of *Livre des Cent Aphorismes d'Hermes.*"[9]

Finally, Leon Lasson proved[10] that the three or four first days of the lunation are extremely fertile, while the last days of the lunar month are very infertile; over a period of about five or six days, the full Moon seems also very favorable for fertilization, according to statistics.

In a direct manner, this confirms the common tradition which says that the increasing Moon hastens marriage and the decreasing Moon retards it.

The Lunar Houses can be divided into four categories:

Unfavorable: I, IX, X, XV, XIX, XX, XXVIII;
Doubtful: II, VI, XIV, XVIII, XXIII, XXVII;
Neutral: III, IV, V, XI, XVI, XXIV, XXI, XXV, and XXVI;
Favorable: VII, VIII, XII, XIII, XVII, XXII.

Before beginning the summary of the nature of these Lunar Houses, we should say in a general way, that enterprises should not be begun or even important steps be taken when the Moon is in an unfavorable House.

"Do not begin quarrels, or hearings, or trials, when the Moon is of a malefic nature, because if you manage it without difficulties, you will lose your case," says an old astrological aphorism.

On the contrary, the passage of the Moon through favorable and neutral Houses must be used to advantage, obviously while not losing sight of the general condition of the heavens and all the other astrological factors.

The nature of the twenty-eight Houses can be described in the following manner:

HOUSE I—The most inauspicious of all, along with the XX-VIII; its nature will be described, with evidence in support of this, in the next chapter.

HOUSE II—The passage of the Moon through this house is good for conceiving a plan and outlining or perfecting a transaction, but unfavorable for the beginning of an enterprise. Thus, it would be advisable not to undertake anything important or public and to protect ideas and plans. According to an anonymous manuscript of 1250, signed by M.A., this Lunar House is nonetheless favorable for the beginning of a journey, for the foundation of an edifice, for crops and planting. Illnesses which break out during the passage of the Moon through this House will not last long and children born here will develop normally and will be strong during childhood.

HOUSE III—Apparently the same as the preceding House, but attenuated. More favorable for private life than for public matters.[11]

HOUSE IV—Gives good hope of success in life, but with patience. The Lunar transit through this House facilitates actions of minor importance and friendly relations. The man who falls ill when the Moon progresses into this House will have difficulty recovering, and children who are born here may die.

HOUSE V—Particularly encouraging to all enterprises somehow concerned with water and the sea, journeys, constructions and search for lost objects. Illnesses beginning here are dangerous. The child born here will be egotistical, reserved, and presumptuous.

HOUSE VI—Threat of deceit or betrayal in a natal chart as well as with the transit of the Moon through this House. Persons born at this time suffer from many deceptions and indiscretions.

HOUSE VII—Weakens health: the child will live only with great care and any illness could be dangerous. But the unfavorable nature of this House from a physiological aspect is balanced by good fortune in material things: it favors gambling, promises support and protection in life coming both from parents and friends, and signifies the possibility of success in the life, but after some difficulties.

HOUSE VIII—a "House of Happiness," since it promises success in the career, gives good health, and favors the personal life. It is good for enterprises of broad scope, promises elevation or an advantageous modification of situation or business matters and generally gives a good familial or conjugal understanding. It makes persons born under its influence affectionate. Illness that breaks out when the Moon is in this House, is generally not dangerous.

HOUSE IX—Generally corresponds to the seventh day after the lunation, which tradition claims was that of the killing of Abel by his brother. It may be assumed that the belief that a crime committed during the passing of the Moon through this House will be punished, and that malefactors will not evade justice comes much more from the association of this day with the first biblical murder than from astrological observations. According to tradition, this House promotes health and the life force, but does not prevent occasional dangerous illnesses in the course of life.

HOUSE X—Does not favor beauty and is dangerous, for illnesses, but exerts a very good influence on journeys. It is the sign of an unhappy life (parental or conjugal) with many troubles from the opposite sex. Generally, persons having the Moon in this House encounter many obstacles in the course of life, see the defeat of many hopes, and are able to arrange a satisfactory life only with great difficulty. Very often the father is the source of recurring problems. According to tradition, this House signifies an end to life not as good as the beginning. Nothing important should be undertaken while the Moon transits this House.

This House, along with the preceding one, is probably represented in mythology by Ceres. They demand from the native a great deal of perseverance and flexibility to achieve a chosen goal, because they do not promote easy success.

HOUSE XI—Promotes longevity in those born under its influence. Illnesses that appear with the Moon in this House could be dangerous at the beginning. It is also the sign of disagreements with some relatives or with the wife.

HOUSE XII—One of the most fortunate of the Lunar Houses, — for the beginning of a project as well as for taking action that does not depend at all on the efforts of the subject, and that is capable of succeeding only by luck. It always permits a person to make headway in the most difficult circumstances. At the moment of birth, this House foretells good fortune and love of travel. However, tradition states that illnesses appearing during the passage of the Moon through this House could become fatal if they are not attended to immediately.

HOUSE XIII—Gives cleverness and ingenuity and favors the emotional life. This House favors health in men more than in women, whose illnesses can be very dangerous (this refers to the natal chart with the Moon in this House as well as the appearance of an illness under its influence, or in other words the chart of an illness). This House encourages travel, and could usefully be selected for a departure; it seems to incline those born under its influence to become expatriates or travel in foreign lands.

It may be assumed that in Antiquity the Houses XI, XII, and XIII were symbolized by the Goddess Diana. These three Lunar Houses generally allow the native to pursue his favorite vocation or occupations. He may occasionally be cruel (depending on other astrological factors) but he is always fortunate in life.

HOUSE XIV—Begin nothing with the Moon in this House. Illnesses that break out under this influence may be long or dangerous. In natal charts, it is the sign of the danger of reversal of situation or heavy losses.

This Lunar House corresponds to the twelfth, thirteenth, and fourteenth days of the Lunar month. G. Muchery summarized the traditional material about the influences of these days of the lunation cycle as follows: [12]

Twelfth day — Preferable to undertake nothing the twelfth day, since it is completely unfortunate. Illnesses will be dangerous. Children could be deformed.

Thirteenth day — Similar to the preceding one, still useful to refrain from doing things that can wait. Better for children, who may attain an advanced age. Dreams are true.

Fourteenth day — On the fourteenth day of the Moon, God blessed Noah and all his family, in reward for the good actions he had done, so it is very fortunate and illnesses will not be fatal. Dreams can be trusted, they will shortly be fulfilled. Children will love their parents.

The Arab list, reproduced by F. Rolt Wheeler[13], states that the thirteenth day of the Moon signifies a very close family and the fourteenth foretells that children will leave the home early, but will achieve some success.

HOUSE XV—Marks a difficult and generally not very happy existence, defects of vision, mediocre health, and very frequently violent passions. It is the sign of a modest situation, or a change of situation, accompanied by losses in the course of life.

This House generally includes the fifteenth, sixteenth and seventeenth days of the lunation (although the fifteenth is often part of the preceding Lunar House). G. Muchery summarizes them:

Fifteenth day — Permits enterprises with modest beginnings, small transactions; favors retail trade. Children born this day will be intelligent and hard working, but often subject to illness.

Sixteenth day — This day is very fortunate for those who sell food; dreams are true, and children born here live a long time. It is good for changing country or location.

Seventeenth day — Sodom and Gomorrah, the two wicked cities famous for their vices in the Old Testament, perished on the seventeenth day of the Moon and expiated all their crimes with a conflagration. Only Lot and his family were saved. Nothing should be undertaken on this day. Discord between spouses, changes for the worst. Children born this day will be tyrannical, arrogant, and stubborn. Reputation suffers.

The manuscript of 1250 mentioned above, states that anyone who falls ill on the fifteenth day should not worry about the outcome of his illness, but that an illness breaking out on the seventeenth day will be enigmatic and dangerous. The list of Arab significations given by F. Rolt-Wheeler attributes bad habits to those born the fifteenth day and little satisfaction with children to those born the sixteenth day.

Lastly, we mention that Robert Anbelain stated in an article[14] that the fourteenth, fifteenth, and sixteenth days of the Lunar month especially favor astral travel.

HOUSE XVI—Persons born with the Moon in this House may attain wealth through their own efforts, because they are industrious. The second half of the life will be better than the first. But illnesses beginning under this influence will be long and dangerous.

HOUSE XVII—Favors everything having to do with the emotional life and requests for support and protection, but does not seem to favor the beginning of a project. For persons born under its influence, this House promises much travel; their character is good and affable, which allows them to bear ordeals in spite of all possible disappointments. Illnesses beginning when the Moon occupies this House are not lasting.

HOUSE XVIII—A sign of bad character or unkindness. Illnesses that begin under this influence may be long. But this House is favorable for all sorts of projects.

HOUSE XIX—Indicates a patient, industrious person who draws to himself the good will and protection of his superiors. But this House is unfavorable for wealth and the beginning of illness; it causes a lot of worry in the course of life.

HOUSE XX—Failure awaits everything begun when the Moon is in this House. It is wise not to undertake anything, to be careful of one's words, and not to revive old problems. This House brings domestic troubles to persons born under its influence, in the family they make, as well as the one they were born into (in the latter, discord and troubles often come from the mother). Nevertheless this House seems to exert a good influence on the career and facilitates rise through personal merit: it is rare for a man with the Moon here not to win public respect.

HOUSE XXI— Difficult career with long illnesses, and actions by false friends injurious to one's situation. An illness beginning under this influence is not dangerous, but could be long.

HOUSE XXII—For persons born under its influence, it holds much jealousy and envy, especially in the emotional life, but also signifies a certain luck in business and a rising fortune or a prominent position. Illnesses appearing here are generally not dangerous.

HOUSE XXIII—Especially bad in charts of illness. Danger of deceit or theft.

HOUSE XXIV—Sign of insincere relations; consequently, persons with the Moon in this House should avoid excessive frankness. It also signifies a very good change of situation associated with a journey around the age of forty. Illnesses that begin under this influence could prove fatal.

HOUSE XXV—Favors travel and moves, and the beginning of modest projects of small importance. This House imparts to persons born under its influence laziness and negligence.

HOUSE XXVI—Danger of loss of inheritance or patrimony. Good Character. Intelligence.

HOUSE XXVII—Bad for conjugal happiness, especially in feminine charts. The second half of the life may be less happy than the first. All new projects must be avoided during the passage of the Moon through this House.

HOUSE XXVIII—Inauspicious — as we will show in the following chapter.

The Arabs have retained the names of each Lunar day, and it could be imagined that in antiquity each of these Houses bore its own name, like the Mansions. But it is meaningless to try to adapt the Arab names for days to these Houses which don't correspond to them.

Let us apply this information to the proclamation of the Empire of Italy by Mussolini which took place at Rome May 9, 1936, at 10:47 P.M. The chart is on the following page. It will enable us to demonstrate the ease of the calculations that must be made to determine the Lunar Houses occupied by the Moon at one moment or another.

The Sun in this celestial map is in 19° Taurus, while the Moon is in 26° Sagittarius. Since the opposition of the luminaries has already taken place, we must work from the next conjunction of the luminaries, and not the last one.

This conjunction will take place when the Sun is at 29.6° Taurus (this is easy to locate in an ephemeris). At the moment of the proclamation of the empire the Moon was at 26.4° Sagittarius. We must find the distance that separates it from the next conjunction.

$$29.6° \text{ Taurus is} \quad 59.6° \text{ of the Zodiac}$$
$$+360. \quad \text{of the complete circle}$$
$$\overline{419.6°}$$
$$-266.4° \text{ Moon's place in Zodiac}$$

TOTAL DISTANCE . . . . . 153.2°

The table on page 78 shows that 153° before the conjunction of the luminaries corresponds to the Fifteenth Lunar house.

As we have mentioned before, this House *indicates a difficult and generally not very happy existence* and the danger of a *change of situation combined with losses*. To this we may add that the Moon in the Twenty-first Mansion *exerts a hastening and reckless influence —* which could refer to the foundation of the Empire immediately after

CHART OF THE PROCLAMATION
OF THE EMPIRE OF ITALY

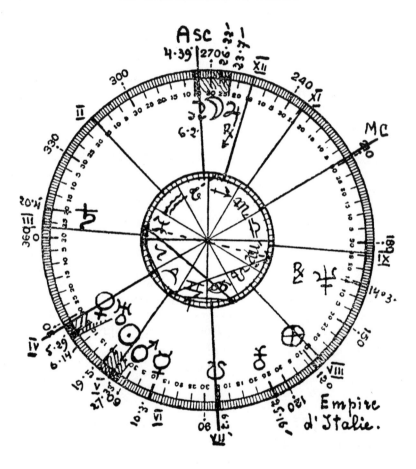

the taking of Addis-Ababa, without waiting for a definite settlement of the conflict.

The Hindus say that this Mansion *favors military men* and we think it is unnecessary to recall that this proclamation took place after a military victory.

The complete interpretation of this chart goes beyond the framework of this book, exclusively devoted to Lunar Astrology. But it is good to remember that if this empire ceased to exist when the Moon by progression arrived at the conjunction with Saturn, it disappeared *de jure* at the signing of the peace treaty of 1913, which corresponds to Hecate in this chart.

NOTES

[1]"Influence de la Lune sur la marche des Maladies," in Le Voile d'Isis, February issue, 1910, p. 33.

[2]Issues 8, 9, and 10 of the ninth year (February, March, April, 1935).

[3]*Planeteneinflüsse,* Constance, 1928.

[4]"La Science Orientale avant les Grecs," pp. 149, 153.

[5]Of course, it is necessary to combine these indications with all the other evidence in the horoscope as is always done in arriving at a synthesis of all the positions and configurations in the astrological chart. As regards the association of humidity, heat, dryness, and cold with the Moon, it is the norm, since this planet plays the principal role in astro-meteorology. All the traditions have left us thousands of rules on the subject, all in need of verification. The Arabs state, for example, that "eleven times out of twelve, the weather during the duration of the lunar month behaves as it did on the fifth day of the cycle, if the sixth day was the same as the fifth. Nine times out of twelve, it is like it was on the fourth day, if the sixth day is like the fourth . . . "

[6]*Le Centiloque,* Paris, 1914, p. 31. Julevno, the translator, adds the following note to this aphorism:

"It must be mentioned that in this aphorism, Ptolemy sets aside the Sun with its individual effect on the spirit and vitality, in order to concentrate on the influence of the Moon, and of its particular action on the moist principle, the Lymph, which makes up the vegetative life of living things or the nourishing juice of the body and which is subject to the increase and decrease of the Moon. From the first quarter up to the middle of the full Moon, when this planet is being warmed progressively by the rays of the Sun, it increases and develops with its influence the nourishing force of bodies. This phenomenon is easily proven by experiment. During this lunar period, hair, if cut, will be imbued with vigor, seeds sown will grow stronger more rapidly, shellfish are fuller, circulation is more active, fevers are stronger, wounds take longer to heal. Conversely, in the waning period of the Moon, from the full Moon to the end of the first quarter, opposite effects are evidenced: plant life loses its vigor, hair grows with difficulty, shellfish are less full, blood flows more gently in the veins, fevers lose their strength, wounds heal more rapidly, and further, a part of a tree, if hacked off will dry out more quickly and will be preserved from rot . . . "

[7]See *Demain,* February issue, 1935, p. 236.

[8]My observations tend to show that this configuration, like all the aspects between the three planets noted by Regiomontanus, only apply in the case of opposition or conjunction.

[9]"Le Livre des Cents Aphorismes d'Hermes," #72 (in l'Almanach Astrologique, 1933, p. 64).

[10]"Fécondation et Fécondité," in *Le Grand Nostradamus,* #17, p. 18.

[11]These interpretations are for the unequal Houses, based on the progression explained earlier. Consequently it is impossible for us to use all the documents pertaining to the daily variations of

lunar influence. Besides, these documents use different numbers of days; the manuscript of 1250, mentioned above, is for thirty days of the lunar month, while the Arab and Touareg lists, given by F. Rolt-Wheeler in his "Cours," number twenty-nine days. G. Muchery published in *Secrets* of March, 1936, a long list of interpretations for each of the thirty lunar days.

[12]"Les Jours Fastes et Néfastes suivant l'agê de la Lune," in *Secrets, #25*, March, 1936, p. 39.

[13]*Cours d'Astrologie,* lesson 66, p.27.

[14]"La Sortie en Corps astral," in *Consolation,* October, 1935.

THE HOUSES OF THE INVISIBLE MOON

Mythology, that wonderful bible of all the traditional sciences, which conceals all the laws of Astrology under the transparent veil of symbols, offers a whole series of lunar goddesses, each one with her own features, which connects each to different parts of the lunar orbit. Earlier, we located Ceres in the Ninth and Tenth Houses, and Diana, in the Eleventh, Twelfth, and Thirteenth. Each of these goddesses symbolizes a particular phase of the lunar influence, and tradition links Houses Twenty-eight and One, those of the invisible phase of the Moon, with Hecate, goddess of the infernal Moon. Of all these associations, this one is most certain, indisputable and unobjectionable. It is also the only one that Greek tradition has transmitted to us, and perhaps the only one it was aware of during the Graeco-Roman period. The attributions of Semele, Rhea, Opis, Cybele, Eileithyia and all the other cosmic goddesses seem to have been already partly forgotten in the classic era; Plato himself admitted that he had no idea what to think of the earlier scriptures concerning the nature of the gods!

What, for example, was the celestial prototype of the lunar Artemis against whom the Ancients beat on cauldrons and made cymbals and brass instruments resound in order to neutralize her magic power—formidable in evil; or else to attract the benefic magic contained in her light? . . .[1]

The first and last Lunar Houses are those of Hecate, *the dark Moon, She who strikes from afar,* who was called *Triple Hecate* and represented by three animal heads. Everything we know of this blood-colored goddess may by analogy be applied to persons born with the Moon in these Houses. Above all it is a sign of much uncertainty throughout life, of feelings which are incomprehensible to the native himself, and of a need for affection which is rarely satisfied.

This plate represents Hecate engraved on a talismanic or magic medallion of the Fourth or Fifth Century, in other words, dating from the Late Roman Empire. The goddess of enchantments and dark rites

is flanked by serpents, and the action of the *Lunar Houses of Hecate in Astrology* is comparable to the treachery of the serpent's bite.

Remember that the poisoner, Hecate, grand-daughter of the Sun, was versed in the inventions of evil: she used wolfsbane to get rid of rivals; she would invite them to delicious feasts and for dessert would pour them a spicy liqueur that quickly brought them from life to death. She did not stop at administering death; according to the myth, she also knew the secret of curious mixtures of herbs that gave hallucinations to those who imbibed them. In perfect accord with this image, this phase of the Moon indicates astrologically a powerful fate in the life which produces strange events, much out of the ordinary and sometimes actually hallucinatory. Later on in this book the reader will find some charts that confirm this statement in an indisputable manner.

But before turning to the inspection of these charts, (which could easily be extended to many others), we should throw some light on the reasons why the especially malefic nature of the dark Moon was not made apparent by all the astrologers who make use almost daily of the conjunction of the luminaries. How could they miss the fatality of this conjunction?

There are probably many reasons for this, the principal one being that the conjunction is larger than the Houses of Hecate: for the conjunction of the luminaries an orb of 12° and sometimes more is allowed; whereas the First and Twenty-eighth Lunar Houses end at 8° 30' from the exact point of the conjunction. In other words, the Moon at a distance of more than 8° from the Sun will fall in the Second or Twenty-seventh Houses whose malefic nature is incomparably weaker than that of the Houses of Hecate. If an orb of 16° or 17° is allowed, the Moon may fall even in the Twenty-sixth or Third Lunar Houses, whose interpretations are different.

THE TRIPLE HECATE

Whose hands hold: destroying fire, a dagger, initiatory fire, and the key that opens the doors of knowledge or those of the regions of hell. A comparison could be made between this representation of Hecate, the only Greek deity with many arms, and that of Shiva, who is also a lunar god.

The Lunar Houses near the point of conjunction allow the conjunction of the luminaries to be divided into different parts; the existence of which is not contested by anyone. In a conjunction with the Sun, most astrologers recognize the phases of *the heart of the Sun,* (which is the true conjunction of the discs), of *cazimi* (within one degree), and of *combustion* (which strongly alters the nature of planets in proximity to the Sun). (It is interesting to note that tradition locates *combustion* at 8° from the Sun, which would coincide exactly with the limits of the *Houses of Hecate,* in a conjunction of the luminaries). These phases are applied to all the planets and not only to the conjunction of the Sun and the Moon. Clearly a multitude of reasons are responsible for these phases being recognized today, including the intra-Mercurial planet Vulcan, but in the case of conjunction of the luminaries, the role of the Lunar Houses seems indisputable to me. In any case, this conjunction is much more mysterious than all the others.

While it is difficult, if not impossible, to find two divergent opinions on the subject of the conjunction of Sun and Mars, the judgments of astrologers concerning the effect of the conjunction of the luminaries are too imprecise, contradictory, and idiosyncratic. We need only open three or four Astrology texts to see that less space is devoted to this conjunction than to other configurations, although its role logically should be greater than that of any other configuration. Very often it seems that writers try to pass over this question without examining it.

Nevertheless, astrologers in every era were aware of the unfavorable nature of the conjunction of the luminaries, without daring to define it. For example, G. Muchery says "the conjunction of the luminaries demands prudence in connection with the (solar) House where the conjunction takes place."[3] H. J. Gouchon considers this conjunction *benefic* (probably because he did not have enough time or opportunity to study it); but he adds, "we must be very cautious, however, as regards the Moon because here, especially when there is an eclipse, the vision is generally defective and the health not very good. In a summary statistic we observed that the position of the Moon close to the Sun (up to 20° -25°) does not seem favorable for longevity . . ."[4]

In this statistic, which is applied to an area widely exceeding the orbit of the conjunction, H. J. Gouchon ventures unknowingly into the realm of Lunar Astrology (which he does not even mention in his "Dictionary"), and enlarges the orb of the devitalizing influence of the invisible Moon. Astrologers have known since earliest antiquity that the Moon conjoined to the Sun, produces a weak and sickly con-

situation, and that the life is generally short if it is ruler of the Ascendant.

In his article on "*Combustion*"[5], Ed. Symours also observed experimentally that "the conjunction of the luminaries seems unfavorable, especially at short distance" for longevity; that it is clearly dangerous, often encountered in charts of violent death; that it seems to damage the faculties of the man of action; and that it is clearly antipathetic to fame.

I should mention that I possess only one creative chart with Hecate: that of Maurice Ravel, born at Cibourne (Pyrenes) March 7, 1875 at 10 P.M.

It would seem Hecate played a particularly tragic role here. The musician, afflicted with a mysterious brain tumor, was not able to compose during the last years of his life; he died during an operation attempted "to relieve his nervous depression" (at the precise moment when the Moon arrived by symbolic progression at conjunction with Pluto).

Eclipses are merely the accentuation of this fatality of the dark Moon. We know that eclipses of the luminaries occurring in the angles of a chart are dangerous. Every astrologer since Ptolemy has reiterated this rule. It can easily be verified that conjunctions of the luminaries play an analogous, though weaker, role; Gaston Doumerge was obliged to abandon his position of power following the new Moon of November 7, 1934 in opposition to his Ascendant and squaring his natal Sun.

There is a second reason why the nature of the conjunction of the luminaries (or the Houses of Hecate, if the Sun and the Moon are not separated by more than 8°) has not been clearly defined: the separation of the luminaries by another planet, a Lunar Node, or even the part of Fortune which "breaks" this conjunction, as it were.

This "break" is not peculiar to the conjunction of the luminaries, it can be observed in all triple conjunctions although this feature is not very well known. For example, if the Moon is in 2° Aries, Neptune in 4° and Mars at 6° of the same sign, the influence of the Moon-Mars conjunction will not be strongly felt; although the question of declination and latitude seem to play a large role.

Apropos of this separation of the luminaries by a third point, we should recall the eighteenth aphorism of C. Ptolemy:

"A person with a benefic planet and the two luminaries (Sun and Moon) in the same degree of a sign in the Ascendant of his natal chart, will be overwhelmingly fortunate in everything he undertakes. The same will be true if the two luminaries are in opposition, one in the Ascendant and the other in the Seventh House. But if it is a malefic planet occupying the Ascendant, it promises extreme ill fortune . . .[6]

As we begin the demonstration of the malefic nature of the Houses of Hecate, we should state that, although these two Houses embody the idea of a fate that threatens in the moment when it is least expected, there is a great difference between the First House and the Twenty-eighth. The Twenty-eighth House is more unfavorable for health than the First and tradition claims that a child born under that influence will be seriously ill during the first seven years of its life and the illness could be fatal. An illness appearing when the Moon progresses into this House is also very dangerous and requires immediate attention.

In any case, the fatality embodied by Hecate seems to manifest itself with more force when the Moon is on the decrease (in other words, in the Twenty-eighth Lunar House), than when the Moon is on the increase. Numerous reasons and observations lead me to believe that the Twenty-eighth Lunar House is even more unfavorable than the First.

As regards the First Lunar House, we should add that if the Sun is in the Sixth Solar House and the Moon in the Seventh, according to tradition, this threatens asthma, smallpox and diseases of the liver.

If the reverse configuration takes place, i.e., if the Moon progresses into the Twenty-eighth Lunar House, and occupies the Sixth Solar House, while the Sun is in the Seventh, this indicates delay in marriage due to pride, as well as diseases of the eyes.[7]

The totality of the horoscope, the general disposition of the planets, the Solar House, and even the Mansion in which the dark Moon is located determine the area in which the malefic nature of the Houses of Hecate will be manifested. Our selection of horoscopes will give an idea of the variety of these manifestations.

The first chart is that of Landru, a rather famous chart since it has been published several times; it is characteristic of the influence of the dark Moon. There have been frequent attempts to represent the modern Bluebeard as a cold calculating person committing his crimes solely to gain possession of the fortunes of his "fiancées." But Hecate in the Twelfth Solar House, that of the subconscious, indicates an unhealthy, disoriented, abnormal psychism, bordering on sadism.

CHART OF LANDRU

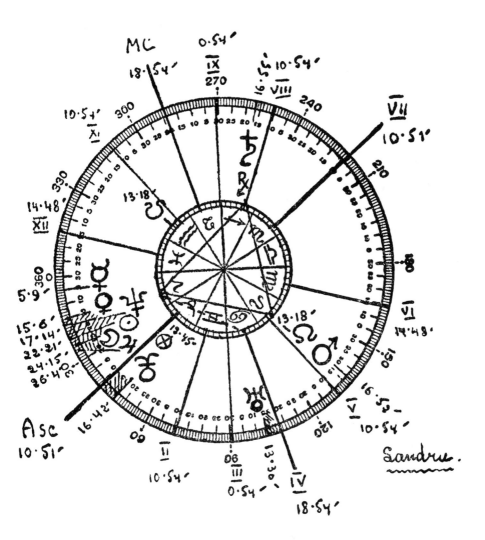

On the subject of this chart, the late lamented, Sylv. Trebucq[8] has said, "A very rapid analysis will reveal the particularly brilliant qualities of the native, disclosed by the magnificent grouping of six planets in Aries.

"The Sun, exalted in this sign, is royally flanked by benefic planets, in very favorable aspect with Saturn on one side and with Mars on the other . . . "

Like Sylv. Trebucq, all the astrologers who have analysed this chart were perplexed when confronted by the number of good configurations it contains. But Hecate covers them all with her sinister shadow.

Let us interpret, for curiosity's sake, the indications given by the position of the Moon in the Zodiac. Landru has the Moon at 24° 15' Aries—in the Second Mansion, one of courage and the will power to direct the native's life by reflection. The Twelfth Solar House, that of crime, clearly shows in which direction the will power will be exercised.

The Hindu interpretation of this Mansion especially emphasizes luck in life; Landru managed to commit his crimes over a long series of years (from 1902 approximately, to 1921), without being disturbed or suspected.

In the Chinese system this Mansion is the sign of "danger of imprudent actions which, like the snare of the trap, paralyze the actions of the native."[9] The Twelfth Solar House is the House of crimes and prisons, the Moon is conjoined with the Sun ruler of the Fifth House of love affairs, and to Jupiter which rules the Eighth House of Death; these indications define the native's actions as being linked with love affairs and death, and indicate his liberty will be paralysed by arrest or imprisonment.

This application of the interpretations of the Second Mansion to the horoscope of Landru may serve as an example for the practical use of this division of the Zodiac.

Before proceeding to the next chart, we should note that the Moon in the First Lunar House and in the sign of Aries is encountered in the chart of Isadora Duncan, strangled to death by her scarf, in the chart of a person burned to death[10], and that of a miner killed in a mine disaster, etc.[11]

Our second chart is that of a wife of a high magistrate, married at the age of nineteen in 1910. The next year, her husband left to go to war and her conjugal life was abruptly ended by this event, because when her husband returned, he did not resume his marital

CHART OF MADAME X.

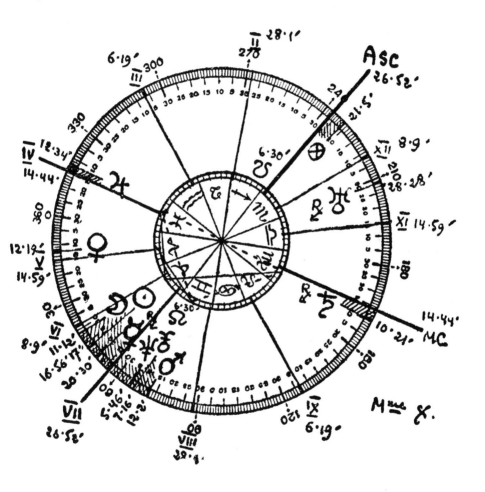

responsibilities. The husband, with a triple conjunction of Neptune, Pluto, and Mars, had many undisguised love affairs; for the purpose of divorce the native was able to assemble evidence of thirteen successive affairs.

At the age of thirty-one she found a true affection that lasted more than twelve years. But a scandal made her suffer much in her thirty-seventh year.

Up to this point, we remain in the realm of more or less banal existence which conforms perfectly with all the known factors of the horoscope, without the necessity of introducing the influence of Hecate. But at the age of forty there began a series of events resembling a gothic novel, or a cinema thriller.

By this time she had long been attracted by occultism and psychism; now she met a Hindu "mage" a hypnotist of rare power, twenty-one years older than herself. Out of curiousity, she lent herself as a medium for his experiments. Very soon he had acquired such power over her that two years later after many attempts at breaking off with him, she left her home without a coat in the dead of winter, in a state of trance, and bought a ticket for an unfamiliar city to meet him; he was waiting at the station when she arrived.

It was this relationship with the Hindu that brought about the break in her relations with her friend and transformed her life into physical and moral slavery.

This chart demonstrates that the malefic action of the dark Moon is not diminished by its exaltation in Taurus; here we have a particularly unfortunate, humiliating, and painful life. Professional discretion forbids me from disclosing more information.

In chart #163 of "*Krankheit und Tod im Horoskop*" an analogous position of the Moon in Taurus did not keep a child from dying at the age of six months; in chart #225, of the same collection, this configuration certainly played a great role in the development of a cancer which led to death. In charts I possess, the conjunction of the luminaries in the tenth House in semi-sextile with Venus, ruler of that House, did not preserve the native from complete ruin. These examples could be multiplied indefinitely.

Among prominent personalities, we find Hecate in Taurus in the chart of Prince Starhemberg, former military dictator of Austria; and since the Moon rules the Fourth Solar House of the end of life, that end will undoubtedly be tragic as a result of his own stubbornness (the sign Taurus and the dark Moon in the First Solar House). He should have serious fears of death by assassination facilitated by the betrayal of his friends.

CHART OF MADAME Y

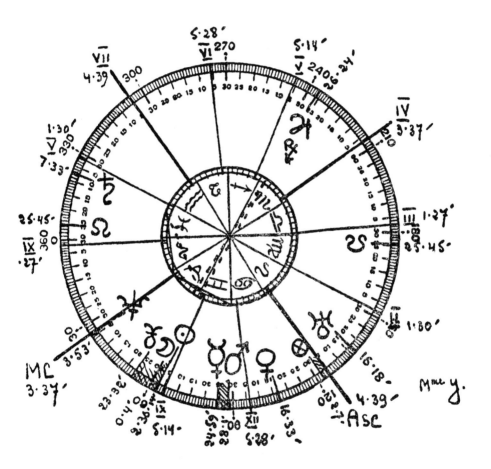

Our third chart is that of a woman from one of the best colonial families; but with Negro blood in her veins, she must inevitably win the hatred and envy of some blacks who will not forgive her for succeeding in white society. Although Hecate is found in the Fifth Mansion, and not the Fourth which is known to have an association with magic, the practice of magic plays a great role in her life, perhaps because of Neptune at Midheaven and Uranus at the Ascendant. Her grandmother died as a result of a curse: her excessively short illness was not diagnosed by the doctors, who spoke of Negro remedies unknown to science; after her death, the putrescent heart of a calf, pierced with needles and wrapped in linen belonging to the deceased, was found in her garden. Frequently the native herself has been the object of attempted curses, and there is reason to believe that she herself has had recourse to unsavory practices.

The presence of Hecate in the Tenth Solar House of social position and station in life, must inevitably produce a downfall, but we would say that the existence of the native has always been unfortunate, weighed down unceasingly by troubles of all kinds.

She belonged to a very wealthy family since birth and her situation was improved by marriage. There are streets and towns that still bear her husband's name. After his death, she found herself responsible for one of the richest estates in the prosperous colony where she lived. But after she moved to Europe, she watched that fortune melt little by little. It has been said that certain relatives are responsible for this (Venus ruling the Third and Tenth Solar Houses in the Twelfth, shows the truth of these accusations). Remember that the Arabs confirm the unfavorable influence of the Fifth Mansion (which contains the Moon) for all sorts of associations; her fortune began to collapse from the moment she combined her interests with those of a distant relative. At present she leads a miserable life, beset with privations.

On page 78 of his "Astrology of Accidents," Charles Carter published the chart of a person who died as a result of beating, and the chart #208 in "*Krankheit und Tod im Horoskop*," is that of a woman who died from cancer; both these charts have Hecate in Gemini.

In any sign of the Zodiac, Hecate seems to predispose the native to cancer, when it does not cause a violent death.

CHART OF MADAME Z

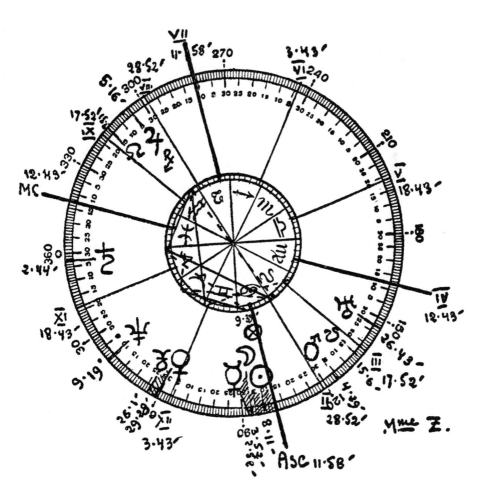

Furthermore, certain writers claim that the conjunction of the luminaries in Gemini makes the native crafty, sarcastic, and not too scrupulous—which can only be explained by the nature of Hecate.

Our fourth example brings us to the sign of Cancer.

It is difficult for me to offer a great many details about the life of this person, born in 1878, because I know only one episode in her life, which was certainly influenced by the presence of Hecate in the Twelfth House, the most unfortunate of all the Solar Houses.

In the beginning of March 1929, after a long illness, death was confirmed by doctors, who gave permission for burial. On March 4, after the funeral service, as the procession entered the cemetery, feeble knocking and cries were heard coming from inside the coffin. It was one of the rare cases of recovery at the last minute (science admits that people buried alive are relatively numerous).

In 1935, i.e., six years after her interment, this person was still alive . . .

Published charts with Hecate in Cancer are quite numerous. Among those charts are those of Mrs. Lindbergh[12] (the kidnapping of her child is too well-known to need recalling); and two cases of insanity cited by Dr. Breteché. My personal collection contains around a dozen unpublished charts. The most interesting of these regarding the fatality of Hecate, is surely that of a marine officer born in Varna (Bulgaria) July 4 (French calendar) 1883 at 1:07 P.M. (local time). In its Ninth Solar House of voyages, this chart has the conjunction of the Moon (10° 3' Cancer), Sun (12° 5'11"), and Jupiter (12° 57' Cancer), a configuration that nine out of ten astrologers will accept as especially fortunate, since Jupiter is exalted and this configuration receives a sextile from Uranus in the Eleventh House. On January 27 1907[14], around 7 P.M. during a crossing from Bulgaria to Odessa, the native accidentally killed his best friend in front of several witnesses.

There are many charts with Hecate in Leo, which demonstrates that the fatality of this Lunar phase is in no way diminished by the presence of the Sun in its own sign. On the contrary, the fiery nature of Leo seems almost to be part of the most outstanding events caused by the dark Moon. The page opposite presents the chart of the aviator Fronval, who was burned to death; the presence of Hecate in the Fourth Solar House which rules the end of the life is characteristic in this regard.

While on this subject we should note that this position of Hecate in the Fourth Solar House is a great danger for succession proceeding

CHART OF FRONVAL

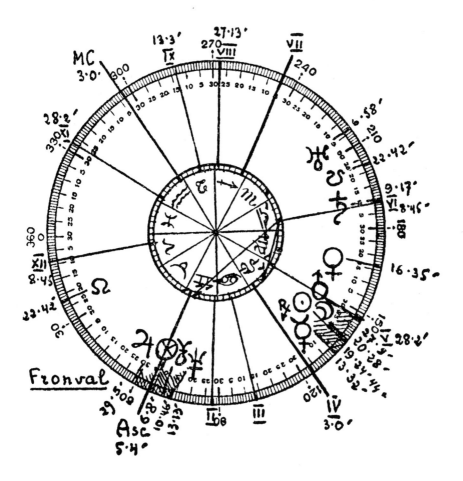

from the father. More than once I have watched what had been a flourishing business under the direction of the father begin to topple as soon as the native took over, and finally, after a series of futile struggles, collapse in bankruptcy. This remark applies to any sign of the Zodiac and not just to Leo.

To return to Leo: M. Edouard Renard, the former governor of French Equatorial Africa, born August 3, 1883 at 2 A.M. in Oran, and killed in an air accident in 1935, also had Hecate in Leo.

It seems likely that this configuration has this effect not only in birth charts, but also in charts of inanimate objects. Further on the reader will see the chart of the largest German steamship *Europa,* taken from a German magazine[15]. This chart was cast for August 15, 1928, 5:15 P.M.

As will be remembered, this ship, which was said to weigh 46,000 tons and to be the most luxurious and fastest ship in the world, was totally destroyed the night of the twenty-fifth of March, 1929 at Hamburg, by a fire which lasted twenty-four hours, and which the inquest attributed to a criminal act.

Hecate confirms this accusation: it is in the Eighth Solar House of death, and the Moon governs the Seventh House of enemies. Furthermore, the Sun is exalted in the sign of the Third House of neighbors and competitors. It could be imagined from these indications, that the arsonists acted on behalf of a competing company.

Of course, we could not say that Hecate always brings death by fire; but the Sun in its own sign by no means diminishes the malevolence of these Lunar Houses. Emperor Franz-Josef of Austria, with the Moon in 22° 29' Leo, and the Sun in 24° 47' Leo did not die a violent death, but his reign was the most tragic of the whole Hapsburg dynasty, because he saw all those near to him die in dramatic circumstances, and watched the collapse of all his hopes.

If the signs ruled by the Moon and the Sun do not diminish the fatality brought by the dark goddess of the infernal phase of the Moon, it is appropriate that other signs of the Zodiac do not change the malefic nature of the Twenty-eighth and First Houses of the Moon.

Louise Barthou, murdered in Marseille, on October 9, 1934, had Hecate divided between Leo and Virgo.

In Charles Carter's collection *Astrology of Accidents,* chart #6, with the Moon in the First Lunar House in Virgo, is that of a woman who was burned; "Krankheit und Tod im Horoskop" contains two charts of insanity with Hecate in Virgo (charts #237 and #325).

CHART OF THE LAUNCHING OF THE *EUROPA*

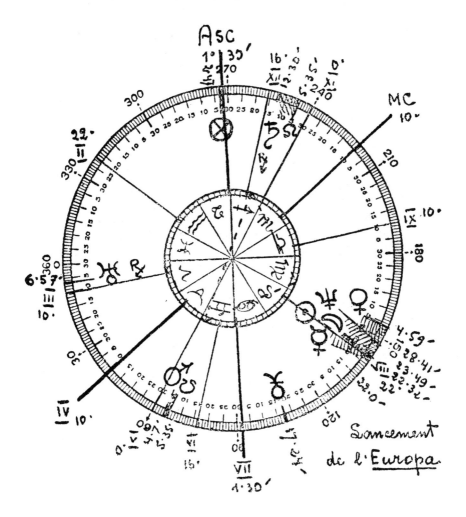

Lancement de l'Europa.

Chart #58 in the same collection, that of the victim of a railway accident, has Hecate in Libra.

In Scorpio this lunar phase is clearly bad for love in a woman's chart.

There is no lack of charts to support these interpretations. We find the bloody goddess in the chart of the "train wrecker" Sylvester Matuska (Hecate in Aquarius)[17]; as well as in that of a case of precocious sensuality[18], and in those of violent death.[19]

On the subject of S. Matuska's horoscope, Conrad Moricand says in his commentaries that the close conjunction of the luminaries in Aquarius always indicates an unhealthy hypertrophy of the ego, so out of proportion that it borders upon the *congestion* of the light, in other words, insanity . . . "

The careful study of people with Hecate in any sign of the Zodiac, may always reveal some psychic anomaly or singularity, even when these people appear very normal and healthy at first glance. At the beginning of this study of Hecate, we said that it imparts feelings which are incomprehensible to the subject himself. These obscure emotions and the subconscious tendencies that it engenders always manifest sooner or later in the life, either in a passing indiscretion, or a hidden vice (Landru and Matuska). The Moon rules the night in general; Hecate symbolizes the murky darkness that hides something shameful or unhealthy. Just as the Sun represented "enlightened mind" among the Cathares (adherents of medieval French heresy), Hecate generally induces one to justify abnormal tendencies by rationalization. The common trait in all those "marked" by the First and the Twenty-eighth Lunar Houses is their amorality, at least in some area. It is as if the shadows of Hecate darkened the solar mind.

This explains why we find Hecate in Leo in the chart of a lesbian, for example, in the collection of Ch. de Herbais de Thun.

It seems to me that the waning of the Moon, or the Twenty-eighth Lunar Mansion has a greater effect on psychism and amorality than the First, but the number of cases observed is still too small to allow us to elevate this remark to the level of a general rule.

Very frequently the rather pathological character of Hecate is so little evidenced in day-to-day life that at first glance the person seems quite reasonable, reserved, retiring, even devoid of emotional impulses. This hidden quality of Hecate explains why C. E. O. Carter says, concerning the conjunction of the luminaries in Aquarius, that it indicates a "cold, capricious and uncertain mind, living in isolation, expressing itself only with difficulty, not managing to adapt itself, its interest remaining concentrated solely on itself . . . " The mind is oppressed, often unconsciously by incomprehensible emotions; when they rise to the surface, or if the person involved manages to express them consciously, they always retain something abnormal and amoral about them.

This state of affairs, which makes people marked by Hecate ideal patients for psychoanalysis, naturally makes them unhappy, like all those whose desires are unsatisfied. Janduz has published[20] the chart of a woman who claimed to have a horror of sexual relations, which she compared to the coupling of animals; this did not prevent her from having four children. In addition she had "vicious and verbally expressed platonic curiosity about erotic fantasies, prostitutes and deviates." This woman had Hecate in Sagittarius, "broken" by Mercury, which considerably diminished its effect. It may be that without this "break" her "curiosities" would not have been confined to the platonic level.

So we can see that, besides the fatality of the life itself, Hecate has a strong psychological effect. Sometimes these two facets of its influences are intertwined and have a unified effect. At other times they appear to be unrelated. The astrologer's task is to determine their relationship in each individual case.

The Moon is generally associated with the Sixteenth Arcanum of the Tarot — *The House of God,* one of the most sinister images; but which aspect of the Moon is expressed here is not stipulated. We have every reason to believe that it is Hecate, who undermines matters in the Solar House where it appears; an undermining similar in every aspect to the image of a tower struck by lightning and decapitated.

These are the results of study of the dark Moon, goddess of Hell; she rides through the world, leaving behind her traces of blood. We will end this chapter with the ancient incantation:

"May the spirit of Lilith not touch you! . . ." Lilith being, among the Hebrews, the incarnation of the same force as the Greek Hecate.

NOTES

[1]According to G. Lanoe-Villène (*Le Livre des Symboles,* Vol. I, Paris, 1935, p. 18.), this lunar magic seems to come from countries north of Thessaly, common homeland of Greek sorcerers, where this goddess was revered as the ruler of lunar purgatory.

[2]P. Choisnard and some other astrologers recommend an orb of $17°$ for the Sun and $13°$ for the Moon.

Robert Ambelain, in the third volume of his "Traite d'Astrologie Esoterique" (Paris, 1942, pp. 74-75) increases this orb to 22° 30' and gives eight different interpretations of the soli-lunar conjunction:

The Moon 22° 30' from the Sun: Changeable destiny. Alternating between good and bad. Irresolute character. Mental disturbance in difficult times. Weak vision. Tendency to rebellion, affrontery. Much travel or at least strong inclination for it.

The Moon at 18° 45' from the Sun: Success in work as subordinate. Rude employees. Bad health. If the Moon is on the increase: accumulation of wealth. If not: bad influence from women; trouble from the mother of spouse. Danger from water.

The Moon at 16° 52' from the Sun: tendency to lying and deceit. Indiscretions committed or suffered which cause much trouble. Engagements and associations broken. Little joy in marriage. Separation or at least misunderstanding. Fluctuation of fortune, succession of good and bad times. Deceit by women or employees. Avoid crowds.

The Moon 15° from the Sun: Good will, benevolent and affable. Good relations with women if the moon is on the increase. Good luck in life. But if the Moon is on the wane, the second half of the life will be less fortunate than the first. Good luck in gambling. Altruism. Will become recognized in the course of his life.

Moon at 11° from the Sun: Changeable destiny. Unstable situation. Alternating gain and loss. Nervousness, feverish quality. Numerous obstacles in one's plans. Incessant setbacks. Envious and jealous people try to work harm. Possible fame or infamy.

Moon 8° from Sun (called Combust): Adversity in life. Diminishes good luck promised by other elements of the horoscope. Increases the danger of bad portents. Strengthens the role of the malefics in the chart. Discord in marriage. Difficulties in carrying out projects. Conjugal misfortune, divorce or death of spouse. Foundering health. Weakness of the eyes. Danger from water (drowning or chill). Tottering situation. If the Moon is increasing: the inauspicious portents are weakened. In an angular House they are aggravated.

The Moon at 1° from the Sun (called Cazimi): words or writings stir up controversy. Protection of important people. Advancement delayed. Obstacles to success, which will nonetheless be surmounted. Possibility of beautiful and fortunate marriage, especially if the Moon is increasing. Hopes for wealth which are realized. Familial happiness. Early marriage. Possibility of infants outside of marriage or adultery for a woman.

The Moon conjunct at 0° from the Sun (called Heart of the Sun): Mysteries and secrets regarding matters of the House in the chart where the conjunction takes place. Secretive, somber turn of thought, eccentricity. Tendency to bear grudges, contained violence. Mind inclined to patient vengeance. Danger brought by the hatred of a woman. Enemies of the opposite sex. In a feminine chart, threat of seduction and abandonment. Danger of traps and calumnies. Illusionary hopes. Very late success at the end of life. If afflicted by malefics, the two luminaries promise: weakening of the faculties, unconsciousness, or amorality. In an angular House: danger from poison or occult practices (hypnosis, potions, spells, etc.).

[3]Dictionnaire de l'Occultisme Experimental, Vol. I, p. 240.

[4]Dictionnaire Astrologique, Paris, 1935, p. 47.

[5]Editions of the Cahiers Astrologiques, Nice, 1946, p.36 and ff.

[6]Le Centiloque, p. 13.

[7]These observations come to us from Regiomontanus.

[8]"Landru et les Astres" in Le Voile d'Isis, 1922, p. 263.

[9]See p. 38 of this book.

[10]Astrology of Accidents, by Charles Carter, p. 57, chart #5. I must thank M. Ch. de Herbais de Thun who brought this chart, among others, to my attention.

[11]Demain, Issue of October 21, 1934, p. 132.

[12]Astrologie, vol. VII, p. 60.

[13]Astrologie Psychologique et Medicale, Vienna, 1935, case #8 and #53.

[14]I do not know if it is Gregorian or Julian calendar.

[15]Die Astrologie, September issue, 1928.

[16]Note that the chart of the launching of the Normandie, given by H-J. Gouchon in "Dictionnaire Astrologique," (p. 110), has Hecate in the Eighth House, but in Scorpio and not

Leo. Scorpio, a water sign, threatens sinking above all in this chart.

Already, June 22, 1936, the crash of the English seaplane on the bridge of the Normandie, had shown that the stars are not at all favorable to it. This was only the first warning of its fate, foretelling the unfortunate end of this super steamship, pride of the French fleet.

We should mention that the conjunction of the luminaries seems to have some relationship with air accidents and in the list of eight accidents given in *Demain* (April 21, 1936 issue, pp. 491-92), three occurred at the moment of conjunction which is a very high percentage.

[17]This chart was published in *Le Grand Nostradamus,* #7.

[18]*Astrologie,* Vol. III, p. 40.

[19]*Krankheit und Tod im Horoskop,* Charts #60 and #103.

[20]*Methode d'interpretation du Belier et de Mars,* Mougins, 1929.

INTERPRETATIONS OF THE DIVISIONS
ACCORDING TO BELOT

_____

"Mr. Jean Belot, pastor at Milmonts, professor of divine and celestial sciences," published, at the beginning of the XVII century, a curious attempt at a synthesis of the "Divinatory" sciences, in which he relied on Raymond Lully and C. Agrippa equally as much as on Gerard of Cremona, thus demonstrating the extent and eclecticism of his scholarship at the same time that he proves the daring and modernism of his ideas. (After all, in one of his chapters he discusses, apropos of physiognomy, "natural markings, their correspondence to signs of the Zodiac and *how we can make the horoscope by recognizing them*.")

He describes, in his work, the meaning of the Lunar Mansions (in the section devoted to chiromancy) and since these attributions are not always in agreement with customary ones, and could have been borrowed from sources of tradition now lost to us, it seemed interesting to reproduce them here:

House

I (Aries):	Ruin of one's enemies
II (Aries):	Reconciliation, short illness.
III (Aries):	Prosperity, good fortune.
IV (Taurus):	Enmity, vengeance, deceit.
V (Taurus):	Favor of great ones.
VI (Gemini):	Loves and fortunate marriage.
VII (Gemini):	Good for acquiring wealth.
VIII (In reality, according to the author, 1st House of the 2nd quadrangle or quarter- Cancer):	Victory for him who undertakes combat.

IX	(Cancer):	Mortal illness.
X	(Leo):	Luxury, fortunate confinement.
XI	(Leo):	Reverence and fear of death.
XII	(Leo):	Separation from admiration.
XIII	(Virgo):	Peace and conjugal union.
XIV	(Virgo):	Divorce.
XV	(Libra):	Acquisition of friends.
XVI	(Libra):	Gain and commerce.
XVII	(Scorpio):	Robbery, banditry.
XVIII	(Scorpio):	Illness, death.
XIX	(Scorpio):	Recovery of health.
XX	(Sagittarius):	Hunts.
XXI	(Sagittarius):	Calamity and affliction.
XXII	(Capricorn):	Flight and exile.
XXIII	(Capricorn):	Destruction and Ruin.
XXIV	(Capricorn):	Fecundity all around.
XXV	(Aquarius):	Affluence and prosperity.
XXVI	(Aquarius):	Desire accomplished with doubt.
XXVII	(Pisces):	Illnesses and assured death.
XXVIII	(Pisces):	Sufferings followed by death.

It is evident that Jean Belot, who on one hand refers constantly to the zodiacal signs and on the other hand speaks of the quarters of the lunation, unintentionally creates confusion, or perhaps systematically and intentionally makes an analogy, between the Mansions and the Lunar Houses—which allows us to understand certain discrepancies discovered between his data and classical data.

It is difficult to comprehend the reasons which induced the author to place the III division in Aries (unless this is to emphasize the traditional rulership with Mars common to the solar sign and the Mansions) and the XXII to Capricorn in spite of the fact that two thirds of these Mansions fall in the following signs.

One might ask, too, if these interpretations do not belong more correctly to the horary or question charts than to birth charts, although sometimes they are equally appropriate there. However, planetary indications very often are identical in all branches—genethliacal, mundane, horary—and who can say why those of Lunar Astrology should be different.

THE HORIZONS OF LUNAR ASTROLOGY

Every astrological undertaking progresses from the general to the particular, and the pursuit of precise details is the chief concern of the astrologer. This research cannot be limited to beaten paths, and our chief concern is the demand for those elements from traditions other than our own which may be useful and significant. An example will show the value of the assistance offered by astrological traditions of the Orient, which are too much neglected in France. Whereas Western astrologers stop at the determination of the nature of each degree of the Zodiac, Hindu astrologers take into consideration the nature of a tenth of a degree.

Lunar Astrology, which has the advantage of being shared by all traditions rather than being just a local astrological system, may be extremely important in the pursuit of exactness. No one will deny the role played by the 144 soli-lunar polarities popularized by Alan Leo, which are merely the combinations of the influence of the luminaries according to the signs which they occupy. The use of the Mansions supplies us with 336 soli-lunar types (12x28), while the variations in the lunar influence according to the distance from the Sun (in other words, the Lunar Houses) increase that number considerably.

An example will demonstrate this more clearly than any theoretical explanations:

The presence of the two luminaries in Aries is considered as an indication of independence and the tendency to rebellion and exaggeration. L. Ferrand, taking his cue from Alan Leo, in his *Traité pratique d'Astrologie,*[1] describes this soli-lunar polarity as follows:

"This combination makes the native lively, active, capricious, restless and fond of travel. The mind is active, the imagination vivid, and there is more intellect than feeling. The native is stubborn, willful and does not like to be ordered around. He will suffer injury to the head, perhaps as a result of accidents. He will act on the basis of his thoughts rather than that of his feelings; the former are more real to him than his emotions. These people are very independent and self-reliant. If they are not sufficiently ethical, and do not know how to control themselves, they will be involved in many deceptions because of their own exaggerations. In general they have vivid perceptions, and a clear and precise mind; which makes them very straightforward in their business dealings, if they are devloped morally. All of these people run the risk of egotism and their future may depend on it . . . "

The use of the Lunar Mansions lends precision to these rather vague indications. If the Moon is in the first Mansion and the Sun anywhere in Aries, the statement that the native will act according to his thoughts rather than his feelings will be irrevocably false. On the contrary, frequently in the course of his life, under pressure of emotion and without much reflection, the native will undertake reckless actions that will bring consequences he will not have foreseen, which will catch up with him and quite often turn his life in an unexpected direction. In each individual case, the aspects and the Solar House will pinpoint the nature of his actions. But if the Moon occupies the First or the Twenty-eighth Lunar House, we can say with certainty that these consequences will not be fortunate, and that these actions will be the manifestations of an impassioned nature.

If the Moon occupies the Second House, the sexual life will be irregular; excesses and indiscretions will be especially associated with travel and change of residence; and most often, the native experiences the pleasures of love far from the place of residence or birth.

My personal observations do not yet permit me to be as exact and detailed about the effect of this soli-lunar polarity when the Moon occupies the first part of the Third Mansion.

Astrological tradition has not preserved the interpretations of all the soli-lunar variations, but a complete list could easily be reconstructed by observation and deduction or by traces and illusions found in religions, superstitions and customs in every country. Certainly the reasons for the dating of Easter belong to the domain of Lunar Astrology; but the allusions in Oriental religions (which have retained their sense of esotericism much more than the Christian churches have) are more numerous than those of Christianity.

Although the next chapter is devoted to Shivaism, examples from that tradition will not be out of place here.

In the *Lingapurana*, for example, Shiva says: "Those who fast the Fourteenth day of the Moon in the month of *Makha* (February), in honor of my *lingam,* and those who on the following night observe the *puja*[2] offering me leaves of *margosa,* will be certain to have a place in the Kailasa (celestial palace or paradise of Shiva)."

This passage (along with other documents), clearly states that the fourteenth lunar day and following night of *Makha,* are of an altogether different nature than all the other moments of the soli-lunar year.

According to the Hindu tradition, it is also the moment of *Taipusan* — pilgrimage generally accompanied by voluntary tortures. In the region of Conjeeveram, it is believed that the act of piercing the abdomen with the points of lances, in honor of Sahanayannar, is closely linked with the pilgrimage of Taipusan, corresponding to the Moon of the Twelfth Mansion (of the Hindu Zodiac beginning with spring, and not of the Hindu Zodiac of Twenty-seven *nakshatras,* i.e., in the Mansion 21° 25'45" Leo to 4° 17'10" Virgo), and tradition everywhere relates that part of the heavens to the abdomen!

It could even be assumed that if the twelve areas of the body on which the Hindus wear marks of caste refer to the twelve Solar signs of the Zodiac, the designs of these marks should be associated with the divisions of the Lunar Zodiac.

Future study of institutions and religious beliefs deriving from the Zodiac will certainly clarify many obscure points, but until that research is done, we will continue to work with the Lunar system, since it offers new possibilities of precision.

NOTES

[1]Montpellier, 1935, p. 75.

[2]Adoration, cult, cult ritual, and especially offerings of flowers, fruits, etc., as opposed to bloody sacrifices.

TRACES OF LUNAR ASTROLOGY
IN SHIVAISM

As we said before, the mystery of the goddesses of Antiquity and of the Orient—each of which symbolizes a lunar phase or, to put it more astrologically, a Lunar House—are still waiting for their Champolĺion. (French archaeologist who deciphered Egyptian hieroglyphics-tr.) It is not yet at all clear to which phase the images of Semele or of Rhea belong, but every tradition can contribute to the reconstruction of Lunar Astrology.

In Hinduism, Vishnu represents the Sun; he is described in Puranic literature and in the Rig-Veda[1] as being in constant movement, like a turning wheel; his ninety chargers each bearing four names evidently refers to the 360° of the Zodiac, divided into four quadruplicities, and to the three hundred sixty days of the year divided into four seasons of ninety days each. Shiva, divine destroyer or rather transformer of the world, is primarily a lunar image. His sacred day is Monday; even today the members of the caste *Lingayats* refuse to work on that day.[2] His role of perpetual transformer of the world seems perfectly analogous to that of the Moon which gives a different face each night from that of the day before and the day to follow.

As is well known, the cult of Shiva embraces a whole pantheon of different gods and goddesses; each of these individual aspects of divinity should refer to a specific lunar phase.

For example, the day of the new Moon is consecrated to the adoration of *Parvati,* the spouse of Shiva. This identifies her with our Hecate, goddess of somber rites, the shadowy Moon of the First and Twenty-eighth Lunar Houses, which we have already discussed at length.

Here we have an interesting comparison. In India *Parvati* is associated with the number twenty-one. On the day of the new Moon this goddess is offered twenty-one threads with a knot in each, and a fan with twenty-one braces. This fan is passed twenty-one times around the statue of the goddess.

Now the twenty-first card of our Tarot is the *Fool;* the image of spiritual unawareness or of the forces of darkness, — the only arcanum of the Tarot (along with the Sixteenth) which is really appropriate to the phase of Hecate!

Parvati symbolizes the invisible Moon, — although she is considered an ideal wife, which at first glance would seem to contradict the comparison with Hecate. But the fidelity to the spouse can frequently be observed with the dark Moon (especially if Hecate is in Taurus or Cancer), and one need only read Kalidasa, the greatest Hindu poet, to find out all the difficulties Parvati had before her marriage to Shiva.

Clearly, it could be said that the feminine projections of the gods (emanations, polarities) are always of lunar substance, but the trinity *Parvati-Sarasvati-Laksmi* always dominates the other divinities, because this trinity is the feminine projection of the Trimurti, the principal Hindu trinity, and from our point of view, Parvati, the projection of the lunar god, occupies a separate position.

Before leaving the subject of the new Moon, we might mention an interesting item: British authorities have noticed that burglaries, which are very common in India, cease almost completely on certain days — those of the new Moon! This is due to the general belief that the days of the new Moon are unlucky in all aspects, even for theft!

Among the Shivaites, the full Moon is consecrated to *Kama,* the Hindu Eros, and the festival of *holi* takes place then. Known in Assam as *Fagwa,* this feast is no longer observed in our time, except perhaps by meals which are usually much richer on that day; but it is valuable to astrologers, because it reveals the Hindu symbols of the Fourteenth and Fifteenth Lunar Houses.

We must remember that when Parvati decided to win the love of Shiva, she was aided in this enterprise by Kama, Rati (Pleasure), his spouse, and Vasanta (Spring), his friend. Shiva turned Kama to ashes with one glance of his third eye. This myth is explained by the fact that each of these deities represents a distinct lunar phase: Kama, the full Moon must disappear to permit Uma the beautiful daughter of Himalaya, to become Parvati, wife of Shiva. In other words, the death of the full Moon is indispensible if the new Moon is to take place.

It is very possible that when the castes originated, at a time when Lunar Astrology was an active system, the castes themselves were associated with specific lunar phases. This explains many local cults with several interesting relics; for example, there is no other way to explain the fact that the Kotas of the artisan caste visit temples only at the time of the full Moon.

The customs and traditions of different localities in India can reveal the individual nature of different lunar days. The Eleventh and Twelfth days of the Moon, which correspond to the trine to the Sun, are considered important and favorable almost everywhere. For example, a woman among the Kurubas, the caste of weavers, separated from her husband for the period of confinement before delivery, would return to the home with her newborn child on the eleventh day after birth; and her husband would choose a name on the twelfth.

The same tribe follows a custom of purification for ten days after each death; this period of purification ends on the eleventh day with a special ceremony performed by the oldest son of the deceased. On this day of conclusive purification, the Moon forms a trine with the place it occupied at the moment of death; and since the Moon rules the "etheric double" — which in the eyes of the occultists represents the reservoir of etheric forces — this trine must relate to the fragmenting of the "etheric double" or to its total dissociation from the physical body.

Lastly, among the same Kurubas, there is *Dassahara,* the feast of the tenth day, associated with the goddess of the hearth *Kalu Devaru.* So besides *Parvati* and *Kama,* Hindu tradition has preserved another definite personification of a fragment of the lunar orbit.

This period of ten days, which corresponds to the first trine of the Moon, is also found among the nomad caste of *Bonthuks* scattered over the regions of Gunfur and of Bellary. The eleventh day after a death occurs among this caste, a cloth is usually spread on the floor of the house of the deceased, and on it are placed leaves filled with food for the shade of the deceased; after this the direct tie with the dead person seems to disappear. This ceremony is comparable to the one mentioned above.

There is still much that could be said on the subject of remnants of the lunar system in the Hindu customs and superstitions, but it would take a whole volume to treat the subject fully. Outside of the realm of folklore, there are traces of the twenty-eight Mansions and the twenty-eight Lunar Houses even in the Mackenzie collection of manuscripts, which speak of the reign of twenty-eight Kings of the kingdom of Kongu, which vanished near the end of the second century of the Christian era; these kings are a type of astrological arrangement of historical events. They are divided into two dynasties: solar (which represents the waxing Moon) and *ganga* (symbolizing the waning Moon).[3] This interpretation is supported by the fact that some chronicles attribute the origin of *Kapous* or *Reddis*[4] (who are still the most important caste of the ruling party of Madras) to the *Yadava*, the race of lunar beings.

All these details as well as many others recounting the traces of Lunar Astrology in Hinduism, are particularly valuable if we recall that the excavations of Mohenjo-Daro and of Harappa show that the cult of Shiva goes back as far as the civilization of the Indus, in other words, three thousand years B.C., even earlier than the dravidians.[5]

NOTES

[1] I, 155, 6.

[2] Arthur Miles, *Le Culte de Civa*, Paris, 1935, p. 127.

[3] We should note that the word *ganga*, also refers to the lunar goddess of the Ganges.

[4] The *Reddi* means king, which makes this caste one of the most characteristic of the great divisions of Kchattrias.

[5] See La Civilisation de l'Indus, Ernest Mackay, Paris, 1936.

A FEW MORE FRAGMENTS
OF LUNAR ASTROLOGY

Lunar Astrology forms a totality so vast that this book could not pretend to exhaust the subject, especially when its author is an isolated investigator, not possessing the means of a Frazer to mobilize a whole team to assemble data he needs, on the five continents.

Thus, without repeating here material published elsewhere (especially in *l'Astrologie chez les Mayas et les Azteques* and in the articles of the magazine *Cahiers Astrologiques* #2, 1946 and #42, 1953), many things remain to be said about the horoscopic division into twenty-eight Mansions and twenty-eight Houses gleaning from left to right.

Obviously, there is no point in bringing together everything we find in the course of our reading, regardless of its relevance, and thus making a book comparable to P. Santyves' *L'Astrologie populaire et l'Influence de la Lune*. But we must add certain items which may help the astrologer.

The influence of the Lunar Mansions and Houses is very real and can easily be verified each day. Ebertin writes that in the case of an illness, an aggravation is often observed at the moment of the new moon, and he recommends that convalescents never leave their bed at the moment of the new moon, but wait till it is past to avoid a relapse.[1] Furthermore, the temperature will rise at the moment of the full moon; this can be prevented by eating fruit at that time.[2]

This observation on the subject of temperature is easily explained by the hot and dry (i.e., feverous) nature generally attributed to the full moon. Indeed we must recall here that although the lunation cycle is like the Lunar Zodiac, there is also an analogy between the lunation and the solar year which imitates, as it were, the Zodiacal one we just discussed at the beginning of this book (in the Preface to the Fourth Edition). Following this analogy, the winter solstice (minimum light) corresponds to the new moon, the vernal equinox (equality between day and night) to the first quarter; summer solstice (maximum light) to the full moon and the autumnal equinox to the last quarter. Thus the first quarter of the lunation is traditionally humid (moist), the second hot, the third dry and the fourth cold. This correspondence induced Francois de Belleforest, for one, to say that "the Moon in the first quarter has the power to soften; in the second to give fruit; in the third to ripen, and in the fourth to preserve . . ."[3]

Before proceeding, we must nevertheless insist that in spite of these rather "secondary" relationships, the Lunar Zodiac begins at the same point as the Solar Zodiac, i.e., at point *gamma*. Documents, like the engraving we will reproduce later in this chapter, testify to that. If Otto Sigfried Reuter (Germanische Himmelskunde, Munich, 1934, p. 524) and a few others claimed that in China, ancient India and Persia the series of divisions began with the Pleiades which the Moon touches in its monthly revolution, it is simply because the arrangement or the propagation of the Lunar Zodiac probably dates from the time when that constellation was located near the vernal point (about twenty-three centuries before our era), in the same way the name of the signs can be dated from the era of their correspondence to constellations bearing the same names.

However, the Lunar Zodiac is clearly much older, because already at that very distant time, the Sumerians no longer explained the name of the star of the night, and utilized an obvious archaism in making the Moon a "Lord of life," and making of her Temple a "House of Light where destiny is decided"—a name which clearly indicates an astrological center.

It is very possible that one day archaeology will provide us with indisputable proof that the Pleiades were used as a reference point for the vernal point, but I confess to being skeptical for several reasons. The Babylonian astrological tablets have been translated piecemeal, often badly (the translator being completely unfamiliar with Astrology) and in obvious bad faith. The subject holds no interest for historians. (An impressive number of "divinatory" tablets, catalogued many decades ago, have not yet been published.) Also, one must remember that Mesopotamia had, besides the "writings of the poor"—the tablets—a "writing of the rich"—parchment, which was in use far in advance of its supposed invention in the city of Pergamum. Several Assyrian bas-reliefs present a scene where the severed heads of the enemy are counted in the presence of two scribes: one writing on a tablet, the other on a sheet of parchment.[4]

There were even two categories of scribes: *dup-shar,* who wrote on tablets; and *kush-shar,* who wrote on hide or papyrus. Now, no Mesopotamian papyrus has survived to our time, but it seems reasonable that the most important and the most sacred things — including those dealing with astrology — were set down on parchment, the Babylonian equivalent of our deluxe editions.

Obviously, more recent material can and should transmit the teaching of ancient times. Certain Hebraic theories clearly derive from Babylon; for example, the one connecting the Lunar Zodiac to the hands of Adam Kadman, the universal man. The number 28, the number of *cHaLaL=life,*[5] is also that of the phalanges of the two hands; the right hand which blesses is related to the waxing Moon; and the left hand which hurls curses, to the fourteen Houses of the waning Moon.[6]

Like the Zodiac degrees, the Lunar Mansions and the Houses were probably at one time represented by symbolic images lending themselves to multiple interpretations. (Is not pictorial symbolism richer and more evocative to the intuition of the astrologer than a description of influence? The lunar image addressing itself to the subconscious must be so much older than the solar clarity of a precise sentence!) It is only recently that people have begun to record their particular nature with words, though in a distinctly fractured manner. Several complete series of these symbols have survived to our day.

Documents[7] recently published, which derive from Byzantine manuscripts, describe these symbols in detail. Here are some fragments (in hope that an astrologer knowing Byzantine Greek will someday give us an integral translation):

MANSION I — *Horns of the Ram* = *Sourtain.* Image: Two women who make signs to each other (who look at each other) arrayed in a *stola.* Their clothing is scarlet to the girdle; the rest is blue.

This double color allows an interpretation of this Division as superficially martial (scarlet on top), with a lunar emotive basis (blue on bottom); hence sentimental and impulsive outbursts of short duration, without perseverance. Ambition and the desire to appear and "make a showing" (clothing) are betrayed by the "signs" which the two women are making to each other. There is no sustained and fertile activity (work is not done with the "Horns of the Ram").

This is a practical example of what can be drawn from this

image, which could of course lend itself to many other interpretations.

MANSION XVI — *Shoulders* (Flails?) *of the Balance* (Libra) = *Zepaneia*. A body with the head of a monkey, the ears of gryphon, the torso of a pheasant; its tail is spread.

MANSION XVIII — *Heart of the Scorpion* = *Kalp, Alkalb*. A nude female, leaning her head to the right holding her hands over her heart as if to tear it. Behind the heart, a disc sprinkled with stars. (There is also mention of a red object.)

If we want to create a useable body of knowledge on lunar symbolism, we must assemble all the material we can from different sources, collate the different versions and evolve a coherent structure, for which this book is already a solid foundation. Each version appears to have already supplied practical proofs. For example, the mother of the present director of *Kosmobiologie,* Elsbeth Ebertin, who was a traditional astrologer, published in 1929 a list of the Mansions offering some interpretations not existing in preceding publications:

MANSION VI: *Alhanna* (instead of Al Hanach — rarely do two sources give the same name, although almost always the same Arabic root is discernible): Hunt, siege of cities, vengeance of Great Ones, liberation of prisoners. (This last indication does not appear in my book. Now Mussolini had the Moon in that part of the heavens when he was liberated in a memorable fashion by the German parachutists; the Moon was also in that Division on January 24, 1956, when the Sultan of Morocco proclaimed a general amnesty, and on March 9, 1957, when at Rovigo in the south of Algeria nearly four thousand Moslems were granted reprieve from execution in the course of a ceremony presided over by General Huet.)

MANSION XV: *Agrapha* (instead of Algaphia): Discovery of treasures, digging of wells or fountains, provoking of separations and discords, destroying of houses or enemies. (Rudolph Steiner had the Moon in this Mansion and his Goethenaeum was destroyed by fire.)

MANSION XX: *Abnahaya:* Taming of wild animals, extending of captivity, destruction of wealth; this obliges men to come to a determined place. (June 9, 1941, when the Moon was in

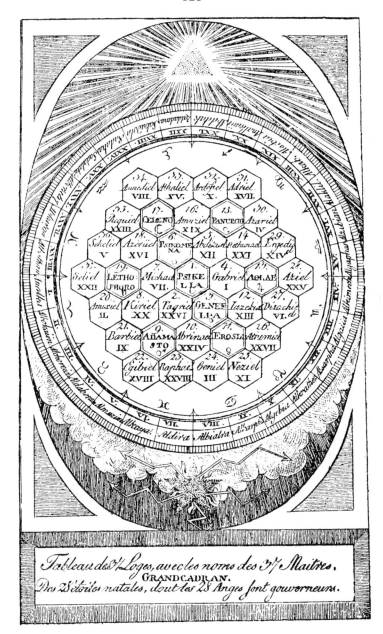

Tableau des 7 Loges, avec les noms des 37 Maitres.
GRANDCADRAN.
Des 28 étoiles natales, dout les 28 Anges sont gouverneurs.

this part of the heavens, was a dark day for German astrology: astrological societies lost everything and many astrologers were arrested.)

There are countless scattered documents of all sorts bearing on Lunar Astrology, but they need to be classified, numbered, explained and even adapted before being put to use. What astrologer, for example, has had the curiosity to open "*Télescope de Zoroastra ou Clef de la Grande Cabale divinatoire des Mages,*" which appeared in 1796 without indication of publishing house,[8] and which the Abbé Barruel in his *Histoire du Jacobinisme* claimed was the formulary of the Masonic lodges? It is generally attributed to Baron Andrea de Nerciat (1739–1800), who was librarian to Hesse-Cassel in 1780–1782 and who, aside from some licentious novels, is the author of the "Urn of Zoroaster" (1793). We took from this book the fine engraving of the Zodiac of twenty-eight Mansions which adorns this chapter.

The signs Virgo and Scorpio are reversed, as the anonymous editors of the book have noted elsewhere.

Two particularities of this Lunar Zodiac merit attention. The author divides the solar year into twenty-eight parts, giving each Mansion a time period of thirteen days sixty-one minutes and twenty-five seconds. This is certainly incorrect, since this time period should depend on the actual time the Sun takes to traverse each section. This Division shows that the particular influence of the Sun in each Mansion was taken into account (which is no longer done these days except in the Orient).

Furthermore, this *Télescope* (certainly on the basis of older documents) attributes to the Mansions different rulerships than are usually encountered, namely:

Mansion	Name according to *Télescope*	Accepted rulership	Rulership in *Télescope*
I	Alnacha	Sun	Sun-Jupiter
II	Albukaim	Moon	Saturn
III	Alkoreya	Mars	Venus
IV	Aldaboran	Mercury	Mercury
V	Albuzin	Jupiter	Saturn
VI	Alkaya	Venus	Jupiter
VII	Aldira	Saturn	Sun-Saturn
VIII	Albiathra	Sun	2 Moons (black & white)
IX	Alkarphes	Moon	Mars

X	Algebla	Mars	Mercury
XI	Alkratia	Mercury	Sun-Venus
XII	Alsarpha	Jupiter	Sun-Mercury
XIII	Algaira	Venus	Venus-Jupiter
XIV	Alkimecht	Saturn	Jupiter
XV	Algaphar	Sun	Moon (white)
XVI	Alzibian	Moon	Moon-Saturn
XVII	Alactil	Mars	Moon-Mercury
XVIII	Alkab	Mercury	Sun-Mars
XIX	Alzebra	Jupiter	Moon-Mercury
XX	Analkaim	Venus	Saturn-Mars
XXI	Abeldack	Saturn	Jupiter-Mercury
XXII	Zaddadena	Sun	Moon-Saturn
XXIII	Sabadola	Moon	Moon (black)
XXIV	Sadahad	Mars	Mars-Venus
XXV	Sadalakia	Mercury	Sun-Jupiter
XXVI	Alporabol	Jupiter	Sun-Mars
XXVII	Alkarga	Venus	Venus
XXVIII	Albothan	Saturn	Mars

For the twenty-eight Mansions, there are only eight common rulerships. Is it possible that the Mansion rulerships are supplanted by the nature of the fixed stars, whose Arab names are transparent in spite of deformation? The double planetary nature of several Houses suggests it, even though the traditional nature of these stars is in no way evident there. Is this the echo of an era where the nature of the Mansion was confused with that of the fixed star marking it?!

I have no fear of being lost in useless detail when I add that this curious and rare book—a veritable cryptogram[9]—is an indisputable proof of the existence in our occidental astrology of *navamsa,* i.e., the division of each sign into nine parts, each governed by a planet. It gives precise useful interpretations for them, other than those of the Hindus. The first verifications clearly demonstrate accuracy.

Returning to the Lunar Astrology of this *Télescope,* we should add that this book counts nine planets by doubling the Sun and Moon, and not by the Hindu method of elevating the lunar nodes to the level of the planets. The so-called "material" or "physical" Moon follows the Sun and can thus be identified with the phase of increase, while the so-called "spiritual" or "moral" Moon precedes the Star of the Day, and is consequently the waning Moon. Furthermore the former is neighbor to Venus and the latter to Mars, which leads us to believe that the Taurus Moon best characterizes the phase of increase, and the

Scorpio Moon the phase of decrease.

Lastly, the waxing Moon should be regarded as a diurnal planet, and the waning one as its nocturnal expression. This question of diurnal and nocturnal planets, so important theoretically and practically, has needed clarification for three centuries now.

NOTES

[1]"I place my faith in the Creator of the World that He may deliver me from the evils which beset humanity, *from the influences of the Moon covered with shadows . . .* " Koran, ch. cxiii.

[2]I must thank M. Henri Latou for having conveyed to me these observations from across the Rhine.

[3]*Secrets de la vraie Agriculture,* Paris, 1572, p. 60.

[4]G. Contenau, *Manuel d'Archeologie Orientale,* Vol. I, Paris, 1927, fig. 85 and pp. 201-202.

[5]According to Mgr. Devoucoux, "Etude d'Archeologie Traditionelle," reproduced by Etudes Traditionelles, #312, December 1953.

[6]The fact that the exemplary lunar number among the Assyro-Babylonians was 30 rather than 28 does not contradict the Babylonian origin of these concepts — these planetary numbers probably belong to another design. Thus for example, Kircher (*Edipus Egyptiacus,* Vol. II, p. 305) and, following him, Lenain (*Le Science Cabalistique,* Amiens, 1823, pp. 119-125), count twenty-eight Lunar Mansions/Houses which they then add the two supplementary days to arrive at thirty.

We must recall that among the Assyro-Babylonians the sign for month was simply the sign for day bearing the number 30, that of Sin, the Moon god. Each planet-deity had his number. Anu, the father of the gods, had the number 60, the perfect number in the sexagesimal system and number of the 60° of the signs Capricorn and Aquarius, over which Saturn reigns in an uninterrupted manner. Bal is assigned the number 50; 40 was the number of Ea, god of the abyss; 15, that of Ishtar. Is it because Venus shows the same phases as the Moon that she is assigned half of the lunar number?

[7]*Catalogus Codicum Astrologorum Graecorum,* Vol. IX, part I, Edition de l'Academie, Brussels, 1951.

[8]According to certain sources, this French edition was printed in Germany. But the *Bibliographie* of Caillet cites, on the contrary, a German translation of *Télescope* which appeared around 1850.

[9]M. Alcor, follower of P.V. Piobb, who brought the *Télescope* to my attention, assumes with good grounds that there is a precise interpretation for each unusual word found there. Thus, for example, if you replace each letter of GENHELIA (name of the solar spirit which opens the series of nine planets) with its following letter, you get: HFOIFMJB, i.e., H(Hiram), Foi (allusion to the eighteenth degree), FM (FreeMasonry), JB (name of the two columns of the Temple). The *Télescope* thus connects Masonic teaching with Astrology, which was always a part of the secret initiatory ceremonies of the Society.

CONCLUSION

I will conclude this general description of Lunar Astrology in the hope that this branch of the Planetary Science will attract the attention it deserves.

Astrology cannot be satisfied indefinitely with the present modes of study, and its progress should not consist only of new discoveries, but also of the reconstruction of Ancient Astrology. The dodecatomories and parts, abandoned by modern practitioners, can bring much more clarity and definition; the seven regions of the Ancients could be valuable for the determination of the areas of activity of configurations in mundane Astrology. But among all the forgotten branches of the Planetary Science of Antiquity, Lunar Astrology is certainly the most important. No chart can be correctly interpreted without the Lunar Houses and Mansions.

I hope that every astrologer will take them into consideration, because even the material assembled in this book will help bring definition to any natal or horary chart.

A. VOLGUINE

BIBLIOGRAPHY

Agrippa, H.-C., *La Philosophie Occulte* (1727)

Bailly, *Histoire de l'Astronomie* (1775–1784)

Bigourdan, *L'Astronomie*

Blavatsky, H.-P., *La Doctrine Secrete*

Breteche, Dr., *Astrologie Psychologique et Medicale*

Carter, Ch., *Astrology of Accidents*

Chavannes, E., *Les Memoires historiques de Se-Ma-Ts'ien*

Curtiss, H.-A., *The Key to the Universe*

Delambre, M., *Historique de l'Astronomie Ancienne;* (Paris, 1817.)

Dupuis, J. B., *L'Origine de tous les Cultes.*

Enel, *Essai d'Astrologie cabbalistique* and *Rota.*

Gouchon, H. J., *Dictionnaire Astrologique.*

Guerin, Abbe J. M. F., *Astronomie Indienne,* 1847.

Ideler, *Zeitrechnung der Chinesen,* Berlin, 1837–1839.

Janduz, *Methode d'Interpretation du Belier et de Mars.*

Muchery, G., *Dictionnaire de l'Occultisme Experimental.*

Paravey, Chevalier de, *De la Sphere et des Constellations de l'antique Astronomie hieroglyphique,* 1835.

Piobb, P., *Formulaire de la Haute Magie.*

Ptolemy, Cl., *Le Centiloque,* Paris, 1914.

Rey, A., *La Science Orientale suivant les Grecs,* 1930.

Rolt-Wheeler, Dr. Fr., *Cours d'Astrologie.*

Saint-Martin, L. C. de, or an unknown Philosopher; *Des Nombres,* Nice, 1946.

Saussure, Leopold de, *Les Origines de l'Astronomie Chinoise.*

Schlegel, Dr. G., *Uranographie Chinoise,* 1875.

Whitney, W. D., *Oriental and Linguistic Studies,* "The Lunar Zodiac," 1874.

PERIODICALS

Astrologie

L'Astrologie

Le Chariot

Consolation

Le Grand Nostradamus

La Science Spirituelle

Secrets

Sous le Ciel

Le Voile d'Isis (since 1936: *Etudes Traditionelles*).

Votre Destin

Les Cahiers Astrologiques